THE
HOLY
LAND
AT WAR

THE
HOLY
LAND
WAR

A Journey Through Israel,
the West Bank and Gaza

THE
HOLY
LAND
AT WAR

MARK PATINKIN

THE HOLY LAND AT WAR

© Copyright July 2024 Mark Patinkin

Portions of this book appeared in different form in the *Providence Journal*.

For permission requests, write to the author, addressed "Attention: Permission Coordinator," at markpatinkin1@gmail.com

ISBN: 979-8-9908872-0-6 (Kindle)
ISBN: 979-8-9908872-1-3 (Paperback)
ISBN: 979-8-9908872-2-0 (Hardcover)

Cover by Rhett Podersoo
Typesetting by Mark Karis
Editing by Becky Blanton

BROOKWAY BOOKS

For Ariel, Alex and Zach, of course.

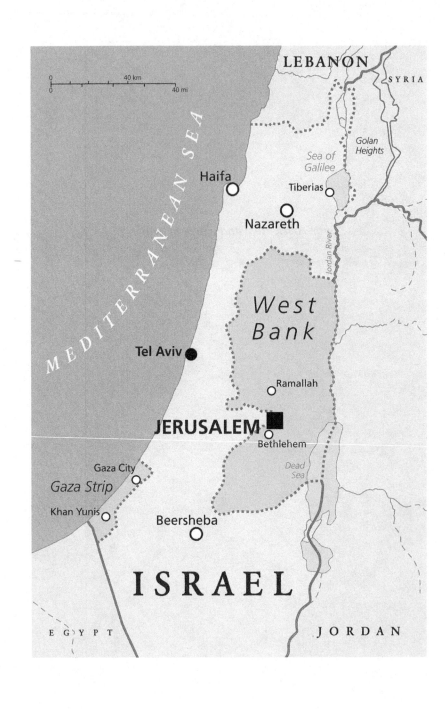

CONTENTS

My first night in Jerusalem, I felt drawn to one of the world's most evocative sites, the Western Wall. (Photo by Bob Ducoff)

ONE

JERUSALEM

I t is my first night in Jerusalem, and though tired from the flight, I feel drawn, as do most sojourners here, to see the Old City, the most soulful enclave I know. And so, after settling into my hotel, I begin the 20-minute walk.

What a beautiful, stunning place, Jerusalem; on almost every block, you can hear the song of history in its ancient streets and limestone walls. Soon, I'm through the Jaffa Gate which still shows bullet scars from the war of 1948, past the Fortress of David, down the narrow path near the Church of the Holy Sepulchre, where Jesus died and rose.

Finally, I emerge into a vast stone plaza, and there it is, the Western Wall itself. Above it, 3,000 years ago, King Solomon, son of David, built the original Jewish temple to house the Ark of the Covenant. It stood for five centuries until destroyed by the Babylonians, the first of 40 conquests of the city, and 100 battles for it.

And now there is another, which is what brought me here as a journalist. The current war, of course, is about Gaza, but in the sweep of history and the eyes of combatants, it can be seen as one more fight over Jerusalem, the seeds of it where I'm standing now, a spot that for millennia has drawn the passions of the world.

It is astonishing to be in the presence of the Western Wall, a wonder both spiritual and physical, running 1,601 feet long and 62 high, its huge limestone blocks forming a tableau accented by growths of Thorny Caper, Black Henbane and Sicilian Snapdragon.

Astonishingly, the blocks extend another 100 feet underground. It was constructed by Herod the Great using 10,000 laborers as a retaining wall for the Jerusalem rise known as Mount Moriah, where Abraham built an altar to sacrifice his son Isaac at God's command.

Scores of Orthodox Jews are praying here this night, and I find a place among them. I am not overly religious, but when you touch this ancient stone, you can't help but ask God for the things you hope for in this world, and a part of you believes that just maybe, this is among the few places on Earth where he is most likely to hear you.

They say the conflict between Arab and Jew is among the world's most complex, but if you look toward the top of the wall, framed by the magenta Jerusalem sky, you also understand its simplicity.

This holiest spot for Jews stands under what is now among the most sacred Islamic sites, the Golden Dome of the Rock built where Solomon's temple stood—all of it yards from where Christianity began. And now you see. For thousands of years, three great faiths have competed over the same few acres, and it is happening again today in Gaza, the Israelis in essence defending Jerusalem and the Palestinians coveting it.

Yet here at the wall, you feel only peace. And then you walk across the vast stone plaza and on the opposite side find a new monument in this hallowed site, a metal plaque with over 1,200 names of the Oct. 7 murdered, lit candles beneath it. Usually, it takes years before a nation starts putting up memorials, but this one-day slaughter was so horrific no one doubts it will stand in Israeli history alongside its many wars—of 1948, 1967, 1973 and the long intifadas.

Finally, the hour late, I head back to the hotel.

But it would not be the only evening I visit the Old City. Later, after a day on the West Bank and on another eve returning from inside Gaza, I find myself passing the Jaffa Gate at just the right moment of dusk when Jerusalem calls most poignantly to the spirit.

Both those days had been long, with hours ahead of me to write, but I couldn't help but pause to take in the ancientness of Jerusalem's center. And so I stood, the Old City's massive walls before me, and beyond them, the minarets and domes, the parapets and spires. I was looking at more than stone, I was seeing half of history itself.

It seems impossible that so much has happened in so small a space. It is where Jesus walked, David ruled and Muhammad ascended to heaven. Even today, it is the holiest of cities for billions of souls.

As I took in the vista, I wondered: if this place calls so strongly to an undevout visitor, what must it do to true believers whose roots run deep in its soil? More than any other place on the planet, conquerors have coveted Jerusalem and subdued it. Romans came and so did Mongols; Crusaders came and a dozen others. They came and in time, most, eventually, were gone.

But two peoples have remained.

The Arab and the Jew.

The Western Wall, the Dome of the Rock, and nearby, the Church of the Holy Sepulchre where Jesus died and rose, are part of a profound convergence of faiths in Jerusalem's Old City. (Photo by Cosmo Condina).

»» ««

I have been a journalist for more decades than I want to count, based with the *Providence Journal* in Rhode Island. Over the years, faraway stories have called, and I've traveled to cover them: a 1980s famine across Africa, a war between Beirut's Christians and Muslims, and the collapse of communism in Eastern Europe. I've reported from Northern Ireland, India and Timbuktu.

But in more recent years, because newspapers weren't as financially able to travel to such places, neither did I.

Then came Oct. 7.

From my desk 5,500 miles away, I began to write about that day. I interviewed a local man who got real time texts from a friend hiding as Hamas invaders killed his kibbutz neighbors. An old high school classmate told me his 50-year-old niece and her husband had been murdered in the attack, their wounded son surviving under his mother's body.

Then, three U.S. college students from the West Bank were shot in Burlington, Vt. while on a stroll speaking Arabic and wearing keffiyehs. The worst injured of them, tragically paralyzed from the chest down, went to school in my own neighborhood, at nearby Brown University.

I reached his American uncle, who told me about the young man growing up in Ramallah, and I thought, what a revealing story it would be to go there and through that lens, see what life is like for Palestinians. And perhaps also, to interview my high school classmate's orphaned nephew about how Oct. 7 survivors are coping. And what, I wondered, is Gaza now like? Would I be able to get inside?

Although part of my job as a columnist is to write armchair commentaries, as I had been doing, a journalist's highest mission is to witness. Was there some way I could make that happen? See the Holy Land at war?

As with most grand plans, at first, it was just something to muse about. Then I learned that others from my home state were on their way. After Oct. 7, the Rhode Island's Jewish Alliance began to hear from local folks asking what they could do for Israel. The answer was simple—go. Be there. So they put together a quick solidarity visit; just three days on the ground.

Twenty signed up, one calling me to ask if I'd want to come along as a reporter. Yes—but my goal was to cover both sides. So I decided to join them for a single day, paying my own way, then staying on alone for a week to report. Except once I got there, seven days wasn't enough. I extended twice, staying for almost three weeks.

As the plane took off for Israel, I was worried about succeeding as a writer. I was told many of the stories I hoped to do would have to be worked out when I got there. That is Israel now—a country in upheaval. The West Bank is similar. And Gaza is a war zone.

At first, because I knew there would be long hours in the field, I planned to write a series about it when I returned home. But I decided far better to send back live dispatches, a daily diary of a region at war. It proved a stressful pace, returning to the hotel mid-evenings and writing past midnight before rising early to head back out. Once I began filing, I finished 13 long stories in 14 days, but there were many experiences—and filled notepads—I didn't have time to get to.

So I pressed on with more interviews back home, where I have woven in another element. Thirty-three years ago, I had also reported from Israel and the territories, at one point patrolling Gaza in an Israeli Jeep targeted with thrown rocks as we drove. I also talked to Palestinians on the ground there, and in the West Bank. I wondered: where are those folks now? I managed to find many of them, each offering a powerful then-and-now perspective.

That is what led to this book, an expanded version of what I wrote from Israel in early 2024 as a first draft of history for my newspaper. As for my parallel journey here decades before, it's an insight into how little has changed. When I reached those same folks three decades later, many said it's as if time has stood still, with Israelis and Palestinians in the exact same dance.

Except the divide is greater.

Perhaps more than any global issue, the current Gaza war has split the world into two camps, with seemingly no middle ground. In my early columns on the subject just after Oct. 7, I was a mostly one-sided advocate myself, defending Israel.

It earned me some choice condemnations, including a Providence Citycouncilman referring to me online as "a disgrace to humanity" and a Brown University fellow calling me "repugnant." Those posts got hundreds of likes.

Two months later, when I wrote that I was heading to Israel, the Brown fellow posted that the idea of me reporting from there was "shameful propaganda"—even before I arrived.

Yet my mission—just as on my 1991 trip—was to be a chronicler, not an advocate, objectively reporting the lives of both Israelis and Palestinians.

Unavoidably, most individual stories I did focused on the truths of just one side or the other. For example, I did manage to get into Gaza with the Israeli army. That article was also published in *USA Today*, my mothership as part of the Gannett newspaper chain, the country's biggest.

A reader named Philippo Vis saw it there and criticized me in an email.

"I just read your story embedded with the IDF from Gaza," he wrote. "Where is the Palestinian side?"

I sent him links to other articles I had written from the West Bank as well as talking to people within Gaza by phone, a difficult task with communications disrupted.

Phillipo wrote back.

"I realized I've judged you too quickly," he said. "Thank you for restoring my faith in journalism as a decent profession."

That message remains meaningful to me.

I don't claim this to be a definitive account. Many journalists have covered the conflict far longer than I, and have more expertise. Nor is this a political analysis. It's just one humble attempt to tell the stories of Israelis and Palestinians I sought out, bearing witness through those touched by war.

My hope is that at least a few readers will feel I've brought them with me.

And that the journey will be revealing.

A worried Akiva Sylvetsky, a Jerusalem attorney, and his physician wife Noa, showed me a photo of their son Evyatar, a 22-year-old foot soldier in Gaza. (Photo by Mark Patinkin)

TWO

NORMALCY AMIDST WAR

We deplane at Ben Gurion Airport on day 100 of the war—except all feels quite ordinary. And then you see them. An endless row as you walk toward the baggage claim—more than 200 kidnap posters, a thing universal here, except these are a bit different, dozens having either yellow or black slashes with Hebrew lettering.

Later I would ask.

The yellow, I was told, means brought home.

And the black?

Murdered.

Such contrast is Israel now, a resilient place, buzzing with normalcy, because that is how Jews here have coped for 76 years, yet this thing that happened Oct. 7, and is happening in Gaza, is always there.

As our bus pulls away, we are told that in the event of sirens, the good news is we're far enough from Gaza that we'll have 90 seconds to get to a shelter, and all buildings here are required to have them. It will be an hour or so to Jerusalem. I look around the bus—most on this trip are older, and I'm surprised they would travel to a nation at war.

Bob Ducoff is typical. He's 78, a retired dentist.

"Israel's in my heart," he tells me. "I want to make a statement to my family on what I believe in."

He's with his granddaughter Sydney Miller, a Boston University grad, and at age 22, the youngest aboard. She'd been to Israel on youth trips, once meeting a young man from there named Hersh Goldberg. He was taken hostage on Oct. 7 at the Nova music festival. There's a video of Hersh being pushed by Hamas into a truck bed, his left arm blown off at the elbow by a hand grenade, bone sticking out as more hostages are forced in next to him with shouts in Arabic of, "Load them, load them." Another video of Hersh would later be released in April 2024 by Hamas, showing him still alive in captivity. He had apparently managed to put a tourniquet on his own arm that day. Sydney is on the trip to stand with Hersh. And also because antisemitic voices in America have deepened her awareness of Jewish fragility.

She tells me her younger brother, a freshman at the University of Pittsburgh, has had to shelter inside when campus rallies made Jews feel threatened.

"I'm glad I'm not at BU this year," Sydney says.

Lydia Fascia-Wong is on the bus, too. She works with children who have autism. Lydia has two kids at home under age 3, but after Oct. 7 she felt a call to drop everything and go. With a Chinese husband and a queer sister, she's been to marches against Asian hate and for LGBTQ rights, as well as BLM, and is miffed that communities she stood with have turned on Israel, and worse. Like Sydney, she's stunned at Jew hatred on campuses.

"I'll never wonder again how the Holocaust happened," Lydia says.

Then there is Bob Alper, a 70ish gentleman who is an unusual mix—a rabbi and stand-up comedian. But he is solemn about why he's come.

"I'm making a shiva call on a country," he says. In Jewish tradition, that's a gathering at the home of the newly bereaved.

>>» «<

Our drive to Jerusalem takes only an hour, despite it being a cross-country trip. People here are obsessed with that, the narrowness of their land, and the price they've paid to hold onto it. Along the roadside, I see unlikely memorials: the preserved frames of armored cars where 2,000 Israelis, some of them Holocaust survivors, died here in the War of 1948. They were killed by Arabs firing from hilltop villages as convoys tried to get supplies to Jerusalem, which was under siege.

Except what was then a narrow, dangerous pass is now a six-lane highway, connecting the Eternal City to Tel Aviv, where they are about to build a 91-story tower in a region that Palestinians claim is theirs. It's as impossible to picture as giving Manhattan back to the Lenape, though Jews point to both the Bible and archeology to insist that here, they are the Lenape.

>>» «<

The contrasts between normalcy and the war have defined my first days in Israel. Mid-evening, I walk down the outdoor Mamilla Mall in Jerusalem, past limestone and glass, Tommy Hilfiger and Pierre Cardin, vibrancy in the air, crowds around me, when I hear a tall, sandy-haired young man saying, "… when I was in Gaza …"

So I stop and ask, and he gives his name as Adam—he's 23, and yes, he was there for two months. And yes, he says quietly, he lost friends.

I tell him I'm an American journalist and might I ask him about it?

He pauses, starts to speak, then says he is sorry, it's too hard.

"Everything you've seen in the media," says Adam, "it doesn't scratch the surface of what it's like."

But he believes in the fight, and if needed, he would be back in it this very night, a physical possibility with the war so close. It's strange to process this as an American, where conflicts for a century have been thousands of miles distant. Here, the front lines are an hour or two by car for most, and minutes for many.

»» ««

On this first evening, we gather at a typical Israeli restaurant, across from each other at a long table. The place is full and lively, and, once again, the war seems far away. I am seated next to an Israeli friend of one of our group, a middle-aged gentleman in business clothes. I ask how he is doing.

Fine, happy to be with you—lovely night.

Then I go there, asking if Oct. 7 changed Israel—and him.

It's as if a cloud has lowered. He says he has not been himself—how could he be—then glances at his phone and tells me he is waiting to hear if his son is OK.

His son?

Yes—he's been fighting in Gaza for two months. The way it works, he explains, is most soldiers aren't allowed cellphones because they could be tracked. Only the commander has one, and when he can, texts his men's parents to say everyone is all right.

My seatmate's name is Akiva Sylvetsky, 57, a Jerusalem attorney with a son named Evyatar, a 22-year-old foot soldier in Gaza. Evyatar was deployed two weeks after the war began. His parents didn't see him for the next two months, and even then, it was just a few days' leave.

You picture Israeli troops in Gaza moving carefully around corners, which certainly happens, the fighting house-to-house. But because of tunnels and snipers, Evyatar spends many hours each day inside an armored troop carrier with nine fellow soldiers. They sleep sitting up, feet between the men across. Once, the air conditioning broke, and it was stifling, but too dangerous to go out. Nor is there such a thing as a shower.

There are 80 or so soldiers in Evyatar's squadron, their parents on the commander's WhatsApp notification group. Israel tends to live on WhatsApp. Usually, texted assurances from the commander arrive twice a day.

On the nights they don't, Akiva sleeps poorly. Friends of his, he tells me, have lost sons.

"We are sitting shiva all over the place," he says.

As we chat, Akiva tells me he at first didn't want to go to restaurants while Evyatar was in Gaza. He even hesitated this night. But he pushes himself to get out, feeling it honors the sacrifice of the soldiers.

"The purpose of what we're doing is so people can lead a sane and normal life," Akiva says.

He adds that others have it worse—a lawyer friend has five boys in Gaza and a sixth up north on the hot border with Lebanon, where 60,000 Israelis have been evacuated due to missiles.

Akiva pauses to check his phone. Nothing.

The last message from the commander, many hours ago, had said simply, "Good afternoon—all the soldiers are healthy"—"shlemim" in Hebrew. Except, Akiva says, "healthy" is not an exact translation. It means more than that.

"How do you put it in English?" he muses. "Shlemim. Wholeness. In one piece, I guess you'd say."

His son wants to be a professor, so once a week, Akiva and his wife send him books on economics and philosophy. There is a lot of time in that troop carrier.

Akiva himself was in Gaza in 1987 during the first intifada—a years-long Palestinian uprising. He remembers stopping a donkey-drawn wagon that was out past curfew and finding two kids around 8 and 12 under a blanket shaking at the sight of an Israeli soldier. They said they were trying to bring eggs to their grandparents.

The moment stays with him.

"No matter what I think politically," Akiva tells me, "or what the solution to Gaza should be—there are civilians there. People suffering."

He considers them victims of both war and their own extremist Hamas leaders.

As someone passes around an Israeli salad with tomatoes, cucumbers, onions and olive oil, Akiva surprises me when he mentions where he lives.

On the West Bank. Technically, he's a settler—what many would call an obstacle to peace. You picture such settlers as fanatics, rifle in one hand, Old Testament in the other, preaching that Jews were here first, over 1,000 years before Jesus—that they've a right to reclaim their ancestral ground. Why else would you build outposts amidst 3 million often hostile Palestinians?

Many settlers are indeed fanatics, but most are like Akiva, mild-mannered professionals who pick their homes the way Americans might choose a more affordable suburb. Akiva lives in Efrat, a liberal West Bank Jewish settlement known for good relations with Palestinian neighbors, established 40 years ago near Jerusalem and now with 10,000 people.

He moved there for economics rather than politics—he was able to own a nice house for the price of a small Jerusalem condo.

"So you're not running around like a crazy extremist with guns," I ask.

"I don't even have a gun," says Akiva.

It reminds of a similar encounter I had on that earlier journalistic trip here in late 1991. I went to a small West Bank settlement of 100 souls called Beit Horon to write about the first intifada—four years of protests, riots and strikes. By the time it was over, 1,000 Palestinians and 160 Israelis had been killed. A second more violent intifada went from 2000 to 2005, with 3,300 Palestinians killed and 1,000 Israelis, many from suicide bombs on buses.

Akiva's home, which he chose for affordability instead of politics, is in a Jewish settlement of 10,000 called Efrat not far from Jerusalem.

I was hosted on that 1991 day by a 40ish mom named Barbara Shamir who moved to Israel from Philadelphia and still had the accent—architect came out as awkateck. Her village of Beit Horn is a four-minute drive from the ancestral Palestinian village of Beit Ur al-Fauqa, where U.S. congresswoman Rashida Tlaib has family.

I asked Barbara if her reason for moving here was ideological—planting the Israeli flag on the Palestinian West Bank?

"It's just a nice place to live," she said. Her kids were free to bike on their own and she couldn't get nearly this much house in Jerusalem. She liked Frank Sinatra and worried about her lawn staying green in the dry climate.

But was this stolen Arab land? Was she a colonizer?

She insisted it was unowned. With much of the West Bank under public Jordanian dominion before taken by Israel in the war of 1967, Jewish settlers, she said, were careful to stay away from deeded Arab property.

"If there was one olive tree," she said, "that was it: the hill was theirs. If there was a goat dropping, we went somewhere else."

The stone floors and good workmanship of Barbara's house made it naturally cool inside on a hot day. Proudly, she gave us a tour, mentioning that most of the contractors were Palestinian.

"We tried to hire Jewish builders," she said, "but they weren't any good. The Arabs were much better builders."

I asked if her town would welcome a Palestinian state. She nodded—yes, most here would. Millions of Israeli-Arabs live in Israel—why couldn't Jews live in the West Bank under a Palestinian government?

Now, as I chat with Akiva in the Jerusalem restaurant, his wife Noa, a doctor, comes over to join us.

I ask them if Efrat has lost many sons in Gaza. Noa nods. Unfortunately, she says, their cemetery has grown.

How do they feel about the angry global reaction to Israel over the war?

Friends who just traveled to Europe, says Akiva, were shocked by the antisemitism. They didn't realize the hatred for Israel is so deep. Akiva tells me it's not the first time in history that Jews have been despised. But unlike previous centuries, they at last have a refuge and the power to defend themselves.

Is he worried Israel is becoming a pariah?

"If we did what the world wants us to do," says Akiva, "we're going to lose. If we don't save ourselves, we won't exist."

Suddenly, his phone buzzes.

Their son's commander.

Everyone, he texted, is shlemim.

The commander's name was Eyal Shuminov. Although only 24, he was already a captain and held in esteem for his unusual maturity. He planned to study astrophysics after the war. Sometimes, he wrote longer messages to the parents of his soldiers.

"It's important you take pride in these fighters," Eyal texted at one point. "Lions, each and every one of them." Those who knew him felt he was bound to be a great achiever in life.

In late February of 2024, weeks after I spoke with Akiva, Capt. Eyal Shuminov was killed in Gaza by an anti-tank missile.

But that night, he was still the lifeline for parents like Akiva and Noa.

Finally, after chatting for a half hour, we say goodbye, and I begin the walk back to the hotel.

The streets along the way are busy and lively.

As is much of Jerusalem in this time when, despite a veneer of normalcy, the war is always there.

I spent a day with a group guided by Geoff Winston, right, with Aviad Reed working security, and learned that like most in Israel, both were touched directly by Oct. 7. (Photo by Mark Patinkin)

THREE

TWO PEOPLES SIDE-BY-SIDE

The next day—the morning after I arrive—we head north by bus out of Jerusalem, past towns carved impossibly into limestone hills. The scenery is stunning but the land difficult, so much so that you wonder why tribes have fought over it since the Bible. The vistas are steep and terraced, a challenging place to build a single house, let alone a country.

Yet somehow, both Jews and Arabs have created worlds here, hewn out of rock, and seeing it, you understand things better. The more you have to sacrifice to live in a place, the deeper your love for it.

An hour-plus into our journey north, we start passing a long concrete wall on our right, clearly a security structure. Our guide, Geoff Winston, tells us the West Bank is on the other side of it. It's a reminder how close everything is here, two peoples wrapped around each other. It is as if geography itself is telling the Holy Land's Jews and Arabs that at some point, somehow, they have to find a way.

Much of the world has condemned Israel for this war, the deaths in Gaza disproportionate to Oct. 7. But studying my phone GPS as we journey, I see us pass a point that explains the obsession here with security—some might say neurosis.

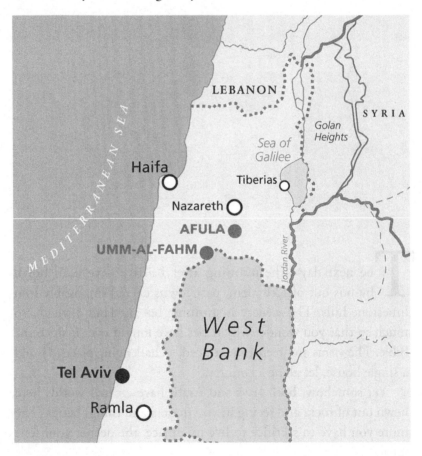

Umm-al-Fahm, a prosperous Arab city, and Afula, are north of Jerusalem and not far from the West Bank.

Our bus is now transiting the country's narrowest neck—an absurd nine miles wide. Forget the river to the sea—an enemy with the kind of vehicles Hamas employed could make it from border to border in 15 minutes, cutting the nation in half.

We continue past a town on our right unfolding up a steep hill, business signs mostly in Hebrew and English, clearly a well-off Israeli community. Except Geoff tells us it's Umm-al-Fahm, a prosperous Arab city, its eastern edge against the West Bank. A decade ago, there was a peace proposal to swap it and similar towns in a land exchange for Jewish settlements, moving each to the other side of an adjusted border. Palestinian leaders denounced it for having the whiff of cleansing. But Geoff tells us that although the folks in Umm-al-Fahm support Palestinians' rights, give them a choice between being Israeli-Arabs or West Bankers and it wouldn't be a contest. They would stay put, as would almost all of the two million Arab citizens here.

This being a Rhode Island Jewish Alliance mission, our journey north is to the city of Afula to see a sponsored youth program and sister hospital. We gather indoors to hear about the first, and once again, I'm struck by how few signs of war there are around us.

And then, there it is.

The youth program director says that in the past, its therapists dealt with the usual span of childhood traumas—family dysfunction and the like. But now she presents a different case, a woman and her 10-year-old son, Yoav. The two were hiding in a home near Gaza that terrible morning when an invader shot her adult nephew in the chest. The attackers moved on, and Yoav watched for hours as his mom tried to stop the bleeding with paper towels. But too much time went by, and the boy saw his nephew's soul slip away, and such trauma has become a new category in this youth program's treatment.

During a "grab lunch," I sit outside by our guide, Geoff. He's 53, and I learn again how almost everyone in Israel was touched by what happened. Geoff's brother-in-law's family lived in a targeted kibbutz. As we chat, I can feel him go from "guide" to human mode, his eyes far away.

"They say they were the lucky ones," Geoff says of the kibbutz, "only 30 were killed."

One of the attackers landed there in a paraglider, and at a critical spot, turned right on a street, walking into the first house and murdering a family. Geoff's brother-in-law, along with his wife and four kids, were in the first house to the left. Had the killer turned that way instead, it would have been them. They survived over the next 10 hours in a security room and for the last 100 days have been among the displaced, in their case in a nice hotel in Tel Aviv.

"And it sucks," Geoff says. "They want to go home, and they can't."

Our group has an armed guard—Aviad Reed, 34. He is carrying a 9mm handgun with two clips.

I ask if he's connected to anyone affected. He answers as if it is an obvious question.

"Of course."

He knows many killed, including soldiers in Gaza, and two kidnapped.

I ask how their families are doing.

"Destroyed."

I tell him I am trying to see a devastated kibbutz, but with so many groups asking for the same, it's hard for even journalists to get in.

When Aviad hears that's my profession, he tells me I need to keep trying.

"The photos don't help," he says. "They don't show the real truth. You have to see with your own eyes."

He was at one of the sites only days before, and says that even more than the burnt-out homes it's the small things that stay with you—like a pacifier still on the floor of a room where a family was slaughtered.

"I've been to Auschwitz," says Aviad, "but this is stronger. It's not cleaned up."

He gets emotional, saying he hopes I'll be able to see because the world is now saying it didn't happen.

"That's insane," says Aviad. "It's obscene."

Our group moves on to Afula's Emek Hospital, sister to Providence's Miriam Hospital, and as we walk the grounds, we come across a curious structure—a sturdy metal cube about 12 feet square, standing randomly by a parking lot.

As the others walk ahead, I stop and ask Aviad what it is. He explains it's a newly placed bomb shelter, and then he gets worked up, telling me there's been a big misconception out there.

All those secure places where Israelis retreated when killers broke into their homes—most were not livable "safe" rooms. They were bomb shelters. No light or air circulation—no plumbing or food. They were meant for 10 minutes of refuge, a half hour at the most. Yet people were in there for 20 hours. And worse—although the heavy doors seal with six connection points where rods go into holes to be blast-proof, they don't lock. The metal hand lever can open from either side.

At that, Aviad goes into the shelter to demonstrate, gripping the inner lever with two white-knuckled hands. This, he says, is how people tried to survive while the invaders twisted it on the outside.

"They held for their life for hours," he says. Except many weren't able to, and imagine, he tells me, the terror when the door was wrenched open, and the shooting and hand grenades began.

His voice rises angrily and echoes against the metal.

"No bathrooms, nothing to eat, stifling air, hours and hours and hours."

We realize we've been left behind, and rush to catch the others at a new building in the hospital complex, six stories of steel and glass. When we go inside, I am surprised to see 50 beds in the basement, 50 more about to be added to the floor below.

I noticed an odd structure in a hospital parking lot—it turned out to be a prefab bomb shelter, a common sight in Israel, where often, there are just minutes to seek safety from missiles. (Photo by Mark Patinkin)

"Why down there?" I ask the head of development, Yaron Sheffer. In America, hospital patients prefer a higher-floor view.

He gives a one-word answer in accented English.

"Bombs."

By which he means missiles. In their case, it's not Hamas but Hezbollah. Now that we've driven a few hours north, the Lebanon border is closer than Gaza.

When I was checking in for the flight to Israel at Boston's Logan, I chatted with a passenger in line behind me named David Shmaya. I asked where he lived. Kibbutz Ma'anit, he said, adding a curious phrase. He said it's part of Israel's "safe corridor."

Meaning?

Just far enough from Hamas in the south and Hezbollah up north that most missiles can't reach it.

And now the light is getting low as we start the long bus ride back to Jerusalem. On various stretches, we see the West Bank border wall, and as dusk turns to night, I find myself thinking again how geography—and history—have sentenced these two peoples together.

And that somehow, someday, there has to be a way.

I interviewed Fayez al Dibs near his home in a West Bank refugee camp. Three of his five sons have been arrested by Israeli authorities. (Photo by Robby Berman)

FOUR

AMONG PALESTINIANS

S oon after Oct. 7, I wrote columns defending Israel, but as a journalist on the ground, I am here to understand both Arabs and Jews, and so I went to the West Bank.

To where Jesus was born.

There is a tendency to think Bethlehem is part of Israel—some picture it near the Western Wall, but it's not like that. It's well beyond the border, an all-Palestinian town with three refugee camps and Jewish settlements encroaching.

To get there, you take a cab out of Jerusalem for a half hour, then walk through a dark, underground boundary tunnel that goes forever, like a subway corridor, pushing through one-way ceiling-high turnstiles. I am the only one here and my footsteps echo. It feels eerie.

But because I'm leaving Israel, there is no checkpoint. Out is fine, coming back in—different story.

The tunnel's so long that when I emerge, I'm squinting into the West Bank sun, and immediately, I'm surrounded by hopeful Palestinian cab drivers. I tell them I'm sorry—I'm about to be picked up.

They wonder why I'm here—few folks have come to Bethlehem since Oct. 7, the war having killed tourism.

I tell them I'm an American journalist. At that, they gather close and want to talk—Palestinians understand the importance of their story being told. Why, asks one, is my government funding bombs killing babies in Gaza?

The others tell him to be careful—he could be imprisoned by Israel for saying that to the press.

"We just wish the war to finish," he says, then adds a line that resonates: "Because no one will win."

He gives his name as Ahmad Joseph, saying he now struggles to support his three young kids. With no visitors, there's no income. Tens of thousands of day laborers here have had work permits to Israel revoked. There has been a surge in Palestinians arrested and shot in Israeli raids. And roads have been blocked for security, turning 30-minute trips into four hour ordeals. And then there are the settlements, which keep growing.

I've only been on the West Bank 15 minutes, and already, I see a core truth of life here. It's about loss. Loss of jobs, freedom, movement, and the most important of all things they will tell you—the loss of land.

Ahmad speaks forcefully, but I don't feel threatened. I hear him out, jotting down his words—that's all he's asking for.

It's also why I'm here this day. With international journalists barred from Gaza, if you want to understand the Palestinian mindset, and heart—and future—you come to the West Bank.

Emerging from a border tunnel into Bethlehem on the West Bank, I ran into Ahmad Joseph and fellow Palestinian cab drivers, who told me life is difficult due to the collapse of tourism and Israel's crackdown after Oct. 7. (Photo by Mark Patinkin)

Yet it's complicated, with the moderate Palestinian Authority ruling here while their extremist rival Hamas runs Gaza. Both territories were briefly under the PA after Israel withdrew from Gaza in 2005. But in 2006, Hamas had a surprise election win, in part because the PA was seen as corrupt. That forced the two Palestinian factions to form a shared government, but it didn't last long. PA leader Mahmoud Abbas, who at 89 is still in power today, began building his own security force in Gaza, which Hamas saw as a coup threat. There was ugliness, such as Hamas throwing a PA leader off a six-story Gaza roof. Not long after, PA people did the same to a Hamas boss. In June of 2007, the two sides clashed in a week-long Palestinian civil war. Over 160 were killed and the PA driven from Gaza, leaving two Palestinian territories with separate governments on either side of Israel.

That put Gaza fully under Hamas, which vowed to kill Jews and reclaim Israel for Palestine. Indeed, they soon began shooting rockets over the border fence and a year later in 2008, Israel had enough and invaded, killing 1,200. In 2014, after Hamas kidnapped and killed three Israeli teens, there was another Israeli-Gaza conflict with 1,800 Palestinians dead. And still another in 2021 with hundreds of casualties. But Holy Land politics are complex. Feeling that a split between the two Palestinian entities was a good thing, Prime Minister Benjamin Netanyahu's government played the game of allowing governments like Qatar to steer money to Hamas. That clearly backfired on Oct. 7.

After 10 minutes of chatting with the cab drivers, it's time to move on. Before I do, Ahmad, who had been doing most of the talking, shares his Instagram with me. Hopefully, he says, we will see each other again when there is peace, Inshalla.

I had wanted to see the West Bank authentically, so instead of hiring a guide, I connected with an average resident, who is now waiting near the cabs to meet me. His name is Omar Zawharah, 39, a Palestinian Muslim and public high school teacher.

As with everyone here, it has been a difficult time for him.

After Oct. 7, Israel, which collects many taxes for the PA, froze West Bank remittances, halving Omar's pay to $300 a month. Others face worse. With the border to Israel mostly sealed, countless folks—mostly construction workers—have lost jobs, their income zeroed out. Palestinians call it collective punishment.

They are not wrong.

Add that to the collapse of tourism, and Bethlehem, whose economy revolved around it, is among the West Bank's most depressed places.

Although Christianity was literally born here with the arrival of Jesus, Bethlehem has gone from 60 percent Christian in 1990 to 85 percent Muslim today, yet Omar tells me its DNA is tolerance.

There is not just one sacred book, he says, but the Quran, the Holy Bible, and, yes, the Torah. Indeed, the first thing he wants to show me is the Church of the Nativity, built on the manger's biblical site, now sitting opposite a mosque.

As we walk through the vast plaza between them, Omar points to a curious symbol of loss—a single pigeon. Before Oct. 7, he says, the square filled daily with thousands of tourists and as many birds. Now, virtually none of either.

I apparently stand out as an American because people start approaching us—first some kids selling rosary beads and now an older man named Kal Yousef. Please, he says—come see what I have for you.

"We love everyone who visits," he tells me, "even if you are Jewish, we say welcome to you."

We follow him to his antiquities store, which indeed includes displays of Judaica. His shop, yards from the church, is a prime location—at least when things are good. No longer.

How hard have these last months been?

"The hardest," he says, "of my life."

Considering past wars and intifadas, it is quite a statement.

Inside, I peruse lovely artifacts, finally asking about a Star of David set on ancient Jerusalem glass.

"For you," he says, "a special price—four hundred."

They use Israeli money on the West Bank since the PA doesn't issue currency, and 400 shekels converts to about $100.

Deal.

But I had misinterpreted—he meant 400 dollars. I hesitate until Omar tells me a similar item might be $1,500 in Jerusalem. I glance at Kal Yousef and can see what it would mean to him.

I'll take it.

He is beyond grateful, telling me it's his biggest sale since Oct. 7.

Kal Yousef brought me to his antiquities shop steps from Bethlehem's Church of the Nativity, where Jesus was born. The war has made business as difficult for him as it has ever been. (Photo by Mark Patinkin)

Omar, though Muslim, wants me to see the Nativity Church, built 1,700 years ago by the Roman Emperor Constantine the Great. It is the oldest church in the Holy Land. We enter from outside through the low "Door of Humility," bending like supplicants, the only ones this day in its magisterial interior with soaring Corinthian columns.

Omar guides me down steps through another truncated door to the small, dark grotto where Jesus was born. It's the world's most ancient site of continuous Christian worship.

I can see how proud he is to have such a place in his city.

We walk back outside, pausing at an overlook. Bethlehem sits on a 2,500-foot plateau and Omar wants me to see the striking landscape below it. We look north toward Jerusalem, Arab villages carved into limestone hills. Yet one element stands out more—rows of newer white homes in a walled Israeli settlement called Har Homa. It was founded in 1997, and by 2003, had 2,000 residents. Today, it's over 20,000.

Omar uses an Arabic word to describe how such Jewish settlements keep expanding on the West Bank.

"Shway, shway," he says. Little bit, little bit.

Omar has arranged for me to visit a friend's home, which is what I had hoped for—to meet common souls and experience the culture.

The friend, says Omar, is a man with five sons—three of them in Israeli prisons. Many families, he tells me, have at least one, with 5,000 West Bank arrests by late January since the war began. And counting.

To meet the friend, we drive into one of Bethlehem's refugee camps, though it's not what you picture. There are no fences or tents. Having been created in 1948, it's now a developed neighborhood blended with the city, a bit scruffy but with big, solid homes made of stone.

Omar assures me the area is safe, and indeed, I have felt no threat on the West Bank although I've yet to see another non-Palestinian face.

One of the other Bethlehem camps, he says, is more radical. "Why is that?"

They have more martyrs—fathers, brothers and sons killed by Israeli soldiers or police. That, Omar explains, is the seed of Palestinian radicalism, and why the cycle continues.

We chat about his work as a history teacher, and his three young kids. He's a lovely man and devoted dad.

Soon, we arrive and meet Fayez al Dibs, in his 50s, the friend with three sons in prison—ages 22, 19 and 16. We follow him up narrow stone stairs to the home's second floor. Fayez needs to pause halfway. He was shot in the calf by Israeli police when he intervened during the arrest of one of his boys. He pulls up his pants cuff to show me the still-purple mark.

We're brought to the best seats in the living room, and soon, seven or eight more folks join us, intrigued that an American journalist is visiting. Gradually, the room gets more crowded—I now count 15. Omar explains it's the culture, with extended families living on different floors of the same large homes. But it's also because Israel limits the perimeters of some Arab towns, so people resort to building vertically on existing structures.

Our many hosts offer Omar and I strong Arabic coffee, then tea, then plates of spiced chicken with rice and nuts. It reminds me of my old-world Jewish aunts when you'd show up unannounced and they'd hit you with enough food for an army.

The meal is mostly for just the two of us, which is Palestinian culture—big families honored to serve a few guests.

As I start to jot some notes, Omar whispers in a polite tone to put my pen down.

"You must eat." One respects one's hosts by focusing on the meal. So I do, and the food just keeps coming.

Fayez, the one with sons in prison, introduces me to two brothers-in-law, and I ask their professions. They were both in construction in Israel, but that's gone now, their work permits revoked.

Women join us, too, all saying the same word to me—I've never been told "welcome" so often.

I ask if they were all born here. Yes, but their patriarch, who recently died near age 100, owned land near Tel Aviv, which they see as their ancestral home.

"But they took it," one says. In 1948.

"They?"

"The Jewish."

You hear this often on the West Bank. Three generations later, they still talk of returning to towns and homes they've never seen. Some have even kept door keys of houses that may no longer be there. I have encountered few cultures where the past is so present.

The aroma of chicken mixes with tobacco smoke—Palestinians, I find, are all about hospitality, food and cigarettes.

A woman named Mona, perhaps 40ish, says she'd like to ask me a question.

Of course.

Why docs my government support what is happening in Gaza? And why seal off the West Bank—she can't go to Israel now for needed health care. Nor can people here pray at the Holy Dome of the Rock.

"They punish us here for what happened Oct. 7," she says.

Yet she keeps offering a smile. Her goal is to pass on a message, not challenge me personally.

One of the men strokes his beard and says it's a new one. Without work, he has let it grow to save money on razor blades. Since the war began, they tell me, there are a lot more beards on the West Bank.

Soon more folks come in—20 in the room now. Palestinian culture is beginning to feel like an episode of "Friends."

Laughing, I ask where everyone's arriving from.

"Family, family, family," explains one of the women. Close friends, she tells me, count as part of that.

I turn to Fayez to ask about his sons. He shows me a phone video taken from an upper floor of one son being led off by soldiers in a night raid. Fayez thinks the arrest was related to Facebook posts—Israel has cracked down on those if they are deemed radical. But families often aren't told the reason. That can continue for months or more—no communication or visits with the imprisoned.

The arrested sons, he says, were at a point of beginning to help support him, a Palestinian custom, and now he's lost that, an especially hard thing since his work as an electrician in Israel has been cut off.

Omar and I linger for over an hour because that's the culture too, but when it is at last time to go, one of the warmest goodbyes is from Mona, who had hit me with the toughest questions. She hopes we'll meet again.

She reminds me of another Palestinian woman I met during that 1991 trip to Israel and the territories. I interviewed her in Gaza, at a refugee camp in Rafah, where today war-displaced Palestinians are crowded into tents.

Her name was Rokaya Al-Najar, in her late 50s, and I can picture her still—her face unlined, but if you looked close at her eyes, you saw someone much older. She offered me tea and pointed to a wall photo of her son Taraq in front of the goldenDome of the Rock. I asked when Taraq managed to visit the Dome—hard for Gazans.

He was never there, Rokaya said. But there was a popular photo service where you sit by a backdrop to make it look that way. Images of the Eternal City were everywhere in this home, recalling what Jews have recited over the centuries during Passover from their own diaspora: "Next year in Jerusalem." Now the phrase is in the Palestinian heart.

"He was killed as a martyr," Rokaya said of her son. In Gaza, that usually means being shot by soldiers during the intifada. Yes, she said, that's how he died.

I asked what he was like. Was he happy as a child?

"Thank God."

And a good boy in adulthood, she said, supporting his family, which is what young Palestinian men do.

Was Taraq involved in the intifada?

He had reason to be, Rokaya said: his father was jailed and his cousin killed. It's what Omar had told me about Palestinian territories today—every time someone is arrested or worse, many in the family are radicalized.

I met Rokaya Al-Najar in 1991 in a Gaza refugee camp, where she held up a photo of her late son Taraq, shot by Israeli soldiers during the intifada. "He was killed as a martyr," Rokyaya said. (Photo by Mark Patinkin)

Rokaya was born in a Palestinian village south of Tel Aviv called Yibna, but she said the Jews pushed everyone out in the 1948 war, when she was 17. Most in her area fled to Gaza, and decades later, she still hopes to go back. The Jews, she said, being an historically exiled people, should understand.

I pointed out that many Palestinians left their homes willingly during the '48 war, so that the Arab armies could sweep in.

No, Rokaya said, they fled for fear they'd be killed by Jewish forces.

"I saw it myself."

I asked what should become of Israeli Jews if Palestinians could return?

It would be all right, she said, for the Palestinian Jews to stay— those who were there before 1948. But not afterward. All of them would have to leave.

She stood and took the portrait of her son Taraq off the wall, pausing to wipe her eyes, then asked me if I have children.

Yes, three.

"So you should understand the pain."

And now as I say goodbye to Omar's friends in Bethlehem, I'm struck by parallels with Rokaya's words in Gaza. Just as she yearned in 1991 to return to ancestral land in Israel, Mona in 2024 did the same. For Palestinians, time seems to have stood still.

Omar asks if I'd like to see his own village, 15 minutes from Bethlehem. I do of course, so we get in his car and start driving. Because Jewish settlements have made Swiss cheese of West Bank land, with restricted roads, we have to go through an Israeli check-point. When we're a few cars from the soldiers, I point at some new buildings on a hill to ask what they're about.

Quickly, Omar pulls my arm down.

"Never point," he says. Israeli soldiers have been jumpy since Oct. 7 and from 20 yards away, could mistake pointing for a gun.

As we drive, there are more Jewish settlements than I realized.

"Shway, shway," Omar says again. Little bit, little bit.

Finally, we arrive at his home, in an urban village that covers a hill. His wife, Noor, gives me a carry-away dinner of lamb and stuffed cauliflower leaves in an old plastic ice-cream container. I accept with gratitude, although I'd rather not lug it back. But later, it saves me because it's Friday night and basically every restaurant and store in Jerusalem is closed for Sabbath.

A half hour later, it's dark as Omar and I pull up to an isolated West Bank intersection where I'll catch a bus back from the West Bank. The intersection is in a rundown spot, but as I glance around, something occurs to me. In America, this might be the kind of place you'd see tents of the unhoused, or folks requesting handouts. But not here. Despite poverty, I saw no one homeless this day—not even one person. Indeed, Omar says that doesn't exist on the West Bank.

"We look after each other," he explains.

As if to prove it, he's kind enough to wait a half-hour until the bus emerges from the dark.

I ask if there's an amount I can give him for his day of time and driving. No—he did it for friendship. I give him $200 anyway, and we embrace as a goodbye.

>» «<

Six months later in mid-July of 2024, less than a month before this book was published, I suddenly got a text from Omar.

"We are tired here," he said.

Tired of the closed roads, blocked tax revenues and collective punishment.

"Every night," Omar said of Israeli soldiers, "they come to the villages to arrest."

But there was something worse: the shway shway. It was accelerating. Extremist settlers felt Israel's West Bank crackdown gave cover to grab more territory.

"They took many lands," Omar told me, speaking of recent moves.

"My land," he texted, meaning around his village. "My family land. Everything. Everything."

He followed with a voice message.

"Houses near my home," said Omar. "The next village near to my village." There was no anger, just melancholy.

"Was it land with houses on it?" I texted.

"Some of them, yes," said Omar. "Destroyed the houses. They have permission from their authority to take lands."

All I could say was, "I am so sorry."

And promise I would do the only thing I can, which is to write about it.

Omar Sawharah, a Palestinian teacher, showed me around the West Bank, stopping here at his village, where he holds a nephew while his daughter and two sons gather around him. Nearby, he said, Jewish settlements are encroaching. (Photo by Mark Patinkin)

>>» «<<

And now, at the end of my long day with Omar in January, I bid him goodbye as the bus to Jerusalem pulls up. Once I'm aboard, an older Palestinian on the seat across notices I seem unsure of myself. He doesn't have much English but puts a friendly hand up as if to say he'll help me.

"You go, where?" he asks.

"Damascus Gate," I say.

He nods—he's got this. At one point, the bus stops and people file out. I stay put—it's too soon to be my destination. But the older man motions for me to follow him off. So I do and it turns out it's the border. Everyone has to go through a checkpoint manned by Israeli soldiers, then get back aboard. My passport gets me waved past, and clearly, the others have papers for Jerusalem.

As we continue in the dark, I squint out the window, nervous about exiting at the wrong time. But at each of the next few stops, the older man motions for me to stay seated. Finally, he stands to leave, gives me a supportive nod and tells me, "Next, next."

Indeed, the following stop is Damascus Gate.

A kind West Bank stranger had gotten me through. It's the final impression I'm left with after a day among Palestinians.

So much loss.

But in the midst of it, so much warmth.

Avi Nevel, born in Israel and now living in Providence, shared real time texts with me from a friend who hid in a secure room in Kibbutz Be'eri on Oct. 7 while his neighbors were being slaughtered. (Photo by Mark Patinkin)

FIVE

"THEY'RE SHOOTING AT THE DOOR"

There is this thing that happens when you ask Israelis about Oct. 7. Many take out their phones to show texts in real time from those being attacked that day. It's startling to see the messages, knowing they were the last words sent by the murdered.

Most begin with pleas for rescue—they are hearing explosions, gunfire, and then, perilously close, shouting in Arabic.

"Everyone who goes outside the house gets killed," said one text I was shown.

"They're shooting at the door," said another.

The progression of each string is similar.

"We're going to the safe room."

And then:

"They're starting fires."

When it was clear there was little hope, they messaged to say goodbye.

Such texts were my first direct encounter with October 7. I was shown them by a Providence resident named Avi Nevel, age 70. He grew up in Israel but moved to Rhode Island 40 years ago when his wife Laura, a physician, matched with a residency at Brown University. She's still a gynecologist here, while Avi, after a career in manufacturing, is now a liaison between local and Israeli businesses.

I was given his name when I first decided to write about Oct. 7, reaching him by phone.

Did he know anyone affected by the slaughter?

Yes, a young man named Ben, age 35. Ben had been in a kibbutz named Be'eri, only a mile or so from the Gaza border. Although there were slaughters in many villages that day, Be'eri was the worst hit, with almost 100 killed from a population of 1,100. Another 25 were kidnapped.

As Avi began to tell me about it by phone, he paused and had to collect himself for a moment.

"I'm sorry," he said, "he's a very close friend."

That's when he said he had gotten texts from Ben while the attack was still happening. Would I like to come by and see them?

When we sat down at his home, Avi said Oct. 7 hit a deep place in him. His own parents survived two World War II Nazi camps. His mother Miriam was in Ravensbrück, where 130,000 women were forced into slave labor, many of them gassed. His father was in the Flossenbürg camp.

After being liberated, Avi's mom learned her parents had been murdered in Auschwitz in Poland and her sister in Bergen-Belsen in Germany. So Miriam, along with a million others, ended up in "Displaced Persons" camps. That's where she met Avi's father.

For Avi Nevel, Oct. 7 brought to mind the ordeal of his mother Miriam, pictured here before World War II in her native Poland, and later deported to the Ravensbrück concentration camp in Germany, which she survived.

I asked why his mother didn't return to where she'd lived before the war.

She did—to her village near Krakow.

"They told her, 'Why did you survive? Go away,'" Avi said.

Having nowhere else, Avi's parents settled in Israel when the nation was born in 1948. Avi's dad, David, a chemist, first cleaned streets there, because that was the kind of job available as they built a new country. Sadly, David died of cancer when Avi was 4. His mom supported him and his older brother by running a small dry-cleaning shop.

I asked Avi how he got to know his Israeli pal Ben.

He met Ben in 2018 on a sailboat cruise in Greece as part of an Israeli tourist flotilla. "When you live with someone on a boat for a week," Avi said, "you create nice friendships."

He showed me some of his earlier texts from Ben. They checked in regularly, especially when rockets were fired into Israel from Gaza, Avi asking Ben if he was OK. The reply was always yes. They had grown used to Hamas rockets, which is why each house had shelters.

A few years ago, Avi visited Ben at kibbutz Be'eri. He remembers that trip well, seeing how close Be'eri was to the Gaza Strip. At one point, he and Ben went to a rooftop overlook. That was when Hamas was sending balloons rigged with devices like Molotov cocktails to set nearby Israeli crop fields on fire during the dry season. From their perch, Avi and Ben could see the smoke.

Since that visit, Ben, who works in marketing, had two sons—now 3 and 1.

When Avi heard about the Hamas attack Saturday, he texted Ben in a group chat with others who had been on the Greek sailing trip.

No response.

Finally, around 11 a.m. Israel time, Ben texted back.

"Many terrorists in the kibbutz," he wrote. "Shooting and burning homes. We are hiding in a safe room, shaking with fear. They already riddled the house with bullets."

Ben was inside with his wife and their two boys.

A few hours later, Avi got this text from Ben:

"Houses are burning while people are in their saferooms. There are reports of shooting into the saferooms."

Avi Nevel's close friends survived the Oct. 7 attack in Kibbutz Be'eri, not far from the Nova festival site."

It was agonizing for Avi as long stretches passed between texts. Finally, after eight hours in the room, Ben texted to say that he and his family had been rescued by Israeli soldiers.

But Ben also had two brothers in the kibbutz. One of them survived the same way Ben did. As for the other, the terrorists set his house on fire. The smoke got so bad it began to suffocate them. Ben's brother and his wife somehow hid their young children elsewhere in the home, then came out and were murdered themselves.

It is believed they confronted the attackers to divert them from their sons. Those were the kinds of decisions that had to be made.

The two sons survived. Ben and his wife, Avi told me, will now be raising their orphaned nephews.

"And that's just one story," said Avi.

He showed me more recent texts from another Israeli friend, explaining what post-Oct. 7 life was like in Israel. This was five days after the massacre.

"Today I have a funeral of one of my friends," the message began. "One of my workers—her husband was killed. Friends of ours, the husband was shot, and the wife and the daughter are missing."

With nine million people, seven million of whom are Jews, Israel can feel like a small town, and Avi told me it seemed the whole country that week was going to shivas and funerals.

Then Avi took out an album to show me archival photos of his mother before she went into the Ravensbrück camp. Oct. 7, he said, has made him see such history in a more present way. The pogroms of the 1900 era as well as the Holocaust had seemed from a different world. The Hamas massacre changed that for him, as have voices from anti-Israel rallies celebrating it. Avi's mindset is that it's 1939 again.

Avi's friend Ben is now living in an evacuation hotel near the Dead Sea with his wife, two young sons, and two newly orphaned nephews. They are among over 130,000 Israelis displaced by missiles from both Gaza and Lebanon.

A month or so after talking to Avi, as I began to plan my reporting trip to Israel, I decided to try to visit Kibbutz Be'eri, a key ground zero of that day. I felt it would be powerful to view it through the eyes of a survivor by meeting Avi's friend Ben there. It would have the additional resonance of it being the first personal story I heard from that day.

At the time I met Avi, Ben had asked that his full name be held back because he was still processing the trauma. By the time I got to

Israel almost 100 days later, I assumed Ben would by then be open to sharing his ordeal and show me Be'eri. At that point, people had begun to deny the slaughter happened, and there was a heightened mission among survivors to give testimony as a defiance of that.

Perhaps Ben in time will get to that point.

But after I arrived in Israel, I asked Avi to reach out for me, and Ben told him he was sorry, it was still too hard for him to go back to his home and talk about it, or even share his full name.

It meant I would have to find another way to see Be'eri.

But first, there was a second ground zero I felt I should visit.

The worst slaughter at a single spot that day was at the Nova music festival. An astonishing 364 people were murdered there, and it has become a shrine of sorts in Israel that anyone can visit.

During my first two days in Israel, I found echoes of the war everywhere.

Soon, I would see where it began.

I met Rotem Yaacovi, 24, and Lina Orlov, 23, survivors of the Nova attack, paying respects at a bomb shelter near the festival site where others were slaughtered that day. (Photo by Mark Patinkin)

SIX

NOVA

From the east, the land of Israel begins as desert by the Dead Sea, rising like Tuscany into the limestone hills of Jerusalem, then lays back down to green flatlands near Gaza and the Mediterranean. It's a lovely but now broken part of the country.

It takes two hours to get there from Jerusalem, and I'm driving into it now with a journalist's guide named Robby Berman. He tells me to keep in mind which direction Gaza is—if a siren goes off, we should crouch behind a wall facing it, or even a curb, to shield from incoming.

But most folks here, says Robby, also have missile apps on their phones that channel warnings from the government's Home Front Command department. Robby prefers the "Red Alert" app, and indeed, later this day, while driving home, it starts flashing a rocket alarm while a robotic voice says, "Missile launched." Robby checks the app and sees the danger zone is far away at "Confrontational Line Area Shlomi." That's the other front. It's Hezbollah firing across the Lebanon border, so no immediate threat to us.

"We're fine," Robby says. But he keeps an eye on the apps as we go. That's what living in Israel is like in 2024.

I learned that most Israelis have apps warning of incoming missiles. This one, on the phone of my guide, Robby Berman, sounded an alarm as we drove near Gaza. (Photo by Mark Patinkin)

It is mid-morning when we reach the Gaza envelope, the swath of Israeli towns near the strip. In better times, it's where tourists came each winter to see red buttercups blanket the landscape—where kibbutz dwellers, being mostly peaceniks, welcomed Gazan workers and believed Arab and Jew could be neighbors.

That was the hope.

We pass banana trees covered by netting, then orange groves, and now we're in the envelope's most verdant stretch, lush with the smell of citrus. Many Palestinians lived in this part of Israel before the conflict of 1948 pushed them out, which is what happens in war, but 76 years and three generations later, those now in Gaza, where their ancestors fled, hold onto the dream of return, in part because the United Nations still labels them refugees. It's one reason this goes on. And on.

I have two things I want to see this day. First, the site of the Nova music festival. Then, 10 minutes further, Kibbutz Be'eri, the worst hit of such communities with 100 butchered. They are 10 minutes from each other.

We are within miles of the Nova site when I notice a typical Israeli structure by the roadside. It's a concrete bomb shelter, a dozen folks gathered around it like mourners, so we pull over to join them. The shelter is perhaps 15 feet square, no door, just an open egress with a turn, like a public restroom, except blast-proof. It says a lot about Israel that such structures are everywhere.

Perhaps, in the chaos of Oct. 7, with the sky full of missiles, shelters seemed a logical refuge. But trying to hide in them proved catastrophic. It left those inside unable to run when found by Hamas militants, who then shot them to death inside. In similar shelters, hand grenades were thrown, the wounded then finished off.

The dozen folks visiting this day had stopped in part to pay respects, but there's something else at play too, a sense that witnessing where it happened is a form of honoring the lost.

Outside the structure, I approach two young women—Rotem Yaacovi, 24, and Lina Orlov, 23. They tell me they were at Nova. This is the first time they've been ready to visit. It was too hard before now.

I ask how they survived the attack.

They simply began to run, they say, never pausing, eventually reaching their car and starting to drive away. But unlike others who braked thinking Hamas militants might be Israeli security, and were killed, Rotem and Lina kept going, even as intruders waved them down, then shot at their car.

There's a single big road in and out of Gaza, and although seemingly the best escape, the two young women sensed that fleeing on it was no longer safe, so they turned off into a field. By instinct, they kept doing all the right things, leaving the car behind and running a long time before hiding for eight hours.

"We saw bodies," says Rotem. "We saw burnt cars. We saw everything."

When I ask how they're doing, Rotem smiles and mentions the scene in the TV show "Friends," where Ross is a mess but keeps insisting "I'm fine." That's what Rotem and Lina tell people, that they're fine, even though they're not.

Now, a few miles further, Robby and I pull just off that same highway into the entry parking lot of the Nova site—open fields surrounded by woods. The red buttercups, called anemones, are salted through nearby grasses. As we step out, there's a concussive blast from the direction of Gaza. Robby says it sounded more like the Iron Dome than a war explosion, but it could be either.

There are many cars at this shaded entry lot, and even more a quarter-mile distant, an area that seems to be the main memorial site, where the concert was held, and the attendees murdered.

But we pause where we turned in because there's a food truck serving a dozen or so Israeli soldiers who tell us they're rotating out of Gaza. I approach two of them—Ofek Kirpi and Yonatan Sela Havatzelet, both 22. They carry automatic rifles. They'd been inside a month and a half.

Were they in many firefights?

"It's all the time," says Ofek. The fights are often at close quarters, but much of their job was to fire support mortars, including smoke for cover, flares for light, or explosive shells.

As I entered the Nova site, I spotted three IDF soldiers on brief leave near a food truck—Ofek Kirpi, Yonatan Sela Havazelet and Charlie Lanin. "This," said Charlie, who grew up on Long Island, "is where I'm supposed to be." (Photo by Mark Patinkin)

Another soldier named Charlie Lanin joins us, age 30, born in Riverdale, Long Island, moving here with his folks when he was young. You run across that a lot in Israel—American born folks.

Charlie is studying accounting at Hebrew University, but that will have to wait until the end of the war, whenever that will be. At 100-plus days when I was there, Gaza was already one of Israel's longest conflicts, and no one here feels it will finish soon. Indeed, as I write this, it is approaching 300 days.

Charlie has a one-and-a-half-year-old and a pregnant wife at home, but he is all right with having been called up.

"This," says Charlie, "is where I'm supposed to be."

Jews, he explains, need a secure country to be safe—history has shown it, and last October showed it again. That's why he fights.

I tell them to stay safe and we head back to the car.

"Keep faith in God," says Charlie.

I was struck by the faces on the posters at the Nova memorial site—young people in the prime of life murdered or kidnapped by Hamas. (Photo by Robby Berman)

We drive a few hundred yards forward and are finally at the heart of the site. It's a former parking area turned into a shrine, marked with an array of posters of the lost on metal stakes driven into the hard-packed dirt. With the passing of months, circles of grass have formed around the bottom of each stake.

The faces on the signs are strikingly attractive, their deaths and abductions having happened in their prime. Dozens of visitors walk among them. A few, like the two young women at the roadside shelter, tell me they'd been wanting to visit since Oct. 7 but couldn't bring themselves to do it.

"We didn't have the courage until now," one says.

I approach a group of about 20 around the poster of a young man named Almog Meir Jan, who is among the kidnapped. The group is here from Almog's hometown of Or Yehuda, not far from Tel Aviv, hours away. A woman named Liat Shulhat, the mayor, is leading the visit. She says this is their way of telling Almog that his hometown has not forgotten him.

"He's constantly on our mind," Liat says.

Almog was 21 when he was taken. He tried to flee in a car with a friend but stopped when militants shot at them. By fortune— perhaps—the attackers decided on abduction in his case instead of murder. Later that day, Hamas released a wrenching video of Almog. It shows him from the chest up, with dark hair and a light t-shirt, crouched on the ground in harsh light, looking up at the captors videotaping him. The fear in his eyes is unmistakable. He stares in panic for a few seconds, then covers his face with both hands. Other men in the video had clearly been beaten. From the look on Almog's face, it seems he had too, and was expecting more.

I recall seeing that video after Oct. 7, and being unnerved by it. I assumed the men in it were captured IDF soldiers, and were therefore getting especially horrendous treatment. It was shocking to learn here at the Nova site that in fact, it was Almog Meir Jam, a simple concertgoer.

Almog Meir Jan was kidnapped from the Nova site. The day I was there, a group of neighbors from his home town of Or Yehuda came to visit in solidarity. He was rescued by the IDF six months later in June. (Photo by Mark Patinkin)

Stunningly, almost six months after my Nova visit, in early June of 2024, Almog was one of four hostages rescued in an Israeli raid in Gaza. He is now home.

You can see why they chose this site for a music festival. It's a beautiful area, shaded with stands of eucalyptus. It is quiet this day, visitors alone with their thoughts as they move from poster to poster. Few react to the occasional booms from the direction of Gaza. You get used to it.

After 15 minutes among the pole-mounted images, I walk 50 yards to a nearby stand of trees. They are spaced 20 or so feet apart, not suitable for hiding, and you wonder, where would you run?

The floor of this treed area is covered with finger-sized pieces of eucalyptus bark, peeling off naturally to make way for the new.

The sun is trying to break through a haze, but it's unable to. Up ahead, deeper into the trees, I see some small shrines, like those by American highways where someone was killed, and I go to them.

All have photos with the lifespans of the murdered, birthdates different, but end of life all the same in the European fashion: 7.10.2023.

Despite the knowledge of what happened—that these were killing fields—there is enough peacefulness here that you don't want to leave.

But I have one more stop, to the worst-hit Kibbutz, called Be'eri, only 10 minutes distant. Even as a journalist, it was hard to arrange a tour there, since thousands want to come see. Out of respect, only so many are allowed, so it doesn't turn into a zoo.

I was told I will find the kibbutz just as Hamas left it 102 days before. Except for the removal of the bodies, it has been preserved like that so the world can see what happened.

We head out of the Nova site, through the lush green of the Gaza envelope, grasses dotted with red anemones, on our way to the worst of the attacked communities.

My guide at Kibbutz Be'eri was Nectar Shavit, 26, who survived the attack that killed 100 of her neighbors. She asked that my photos focus on the destruction rather than her face. (Photo by Mark Patinkin)

SEVEN

A KIBBUTZ AT GROUND ZERO

T he first thing you see as you enter Kibbutz Be'eri are the burned homes, but soon you notice something more unsettling.

Hamas wasn't satisfied to just set fire. What wasn't burned was smashed, leaving hardscaped patios in jagged pieces. They did to the houses what they did to the people—first, they murdered, then they mutilated.

You can tell it was once a beautiful community, Be'eri, the kind of small town that promises you'll be safe. More than 1,100 lived here. Almost 100 were butchered.

We meet Nectar Shavit, 26, at the entry gate. Be'eri was her home.

I suppose it still is. She has volunteered to show us what's left of it.

The landscaping is impressive, the plantings around each block giving a sense of being part of nature. There's an emphasis on flowering bushes, and you wonder if you'd be able to smell their fragrance were it not for the aroma of burnt things, even all these months later.

Nectar is quiet, even melancholy, as we walk to a destroyed house at the start of our tour. She tells us it's where her parents had lived. I would later learn this was the first time she had shown Be'eri to visitors. When I ask why now, she says it's because people are denying it happened. This is her way of answering them.

It's also one reason many of us have come. As with all of history's massacres, there is only one thing you can do for the dead, and that is to bear witness.

The home of Nectar's parents was a one-story townhouse sharing a wall with another. It's now burned-out and smashed, half the roof missing. It has been left that way on purpose. Most shrines to massacres have been sanitized, but Be'eri, at least for the moment, is meant to be a testimony rather than a memorial.

The house had an open design, the kitchen and living area forming a great room. Outdoor light comes in through the jagged, half-missing roof. The floor is covered with broken masonry and wallboard. The ceiling over the kitchen is intact but blackened, the foil gone from the cylindrical heating ducts. There are kitchen implements on the ground and canisters on the shelves. I think one has coffee grounds in it, though the soot makes it hard to tell what the label says. Somehow, there is an intact box of Hanukkah candles on a table.

When we go back outside, we see the adjoining townhouse was also destroyed. On the front of it, there are big posters of the couple who had lived there. The father's name was Ilan Weiss. He was 56.

Ilan Weiss, neighbor of Nectar's parents, was murdered when he went outside to confront the attackers. His wife Shiri and daughter Noga were kidnapped. Many homes in Be'eri feature the faces of their targeted residents. (Photo by Mark Patinkin)

Nectar tells us he decided to run through his front door to confront the attackers and was murdered. Then they kidnapped his body into Gaza.

Ilan's wife, Shiri, 53, and daughter, Noga, 18, were also taken into Gaza. At first, Noga hid under a bed watching as her mother was taken. When the house was set afire, Noga climbed outside through a window and hid in bushes for hours. But the gunmen found and abducted her. Both she and her mother were released 50 days later in the initial hostage exchange. Noga's two older sisters, both in their 20s, survived in a secure room in a Kibbutz student apartment where they were living. The family also had a dog named Keshet. Everyone joked that Keshet was the son the dad, Ilan, never had. Keshet was shot and killed by the militants.

There was something about this shattered window in the kindergarten area of Kibbutz Be'eri that captured the horror of the attack, so I stood behind it for a photo of remembrance. (Photo by Robby Berman)

As we move along, I ask Nectar if I can take her picture, but she demurs. If there's to be a photo of her, she asks that it include what Hamas did here. Nectar has black, curly hair tied in the back with a scrunchie. She wears a gray sweatshirt over faded blue jeans. She has yet to smile.

Her parents also survived in a shelter room with her 17-year-old brother, Israeli soldiers rescuing them just before they likely would have been killed at the end of a very long siege.

Nectar was in a different house with her husband. At one point, the Hamas killers knocked but by grace, moved on. Yet Nectar heard shooting and explosions close enough that she kept thinking she would be next.

The people of Be'eri have a WhatsApp text group. That's how they communicated during the 12-hour attack. Nectar kept seeing messages with phrases like, "They're burning my house," and "They're killing my children."

It began at 6:30 a.m., and the army didn't arrive until almost 5 p.m. By then it was dark. And there was still an hours-long house-to-house fight into the next day. In some buildings, Hamas militants had barricaded themselves with hostages. When Israeli soldiers at last came to Nectar's home, she pleaded with them to save her parents. They told her they were trying, but there were many militants and by then, Israeli soldiers had been killed, others wounded, and Be'eri residents had warned by text that their houses were booby-trapped.

It wasn't until 10 p.m. that Nectar's parents were rescued from their security room. They had been in it since 7 a.m. When it was over the next day, as she walked around the kibbutz, Nectar saw the bodies of neighbors. She saw families, but many were missing members.

As our tour continues, we follow Nectar down her block, and then another. At one point, there's a loud explosion from Gaza. Then more, and more still.

I am using my phone's voice memo app to record Nectar speaking. When I later transcribe it, I miss some of her words because of the loud crunch of our shoes walking over broken things.

Be'eri was founded just before the 1948 war, mostly by young Jews who trekked there from Iraq. It was named after Berl Katznelson, an early pioneer who moved from Lithuania to Ottoman Palestine in 1909 to escape antisemitism. As a writer with the byline Be'eri, he pushed for good relations between Jews and Arabs. Right up until Oct. 7, the community was known for that, with a program to drive Gazans to hospitals in Israel for cancer treatment. They even raised a fund to help commuting Palestinian kibbutz workers who had extra needs.

While we move along, Nectar tells us stories from various houses. In this one, just as in the Weiss home next door to her, an 8-year-old girl hiding under a bed saw her mother kidnapped. Then she heard the Hamas people abuse and kill the family dog. Then they burned the dog. Then they began to burn the house. Somehow, the girl ran out a back entrance to the home of another family without being seen.

Nectar continues to point out what happened here and there. This was where several girls were killed, that's where babies were burned. A mother was shot in the head here, the father in the stomach. One neighborhood of Be'eri is called Kerem. Virtually everyone there, says Nectar, was murdered or forcibly taken into Gaza.

Many of the bodies were intentionally burned—not in a house fire, but with kerosene poured on them. Forensics people later determined that some had been burned alive.

Some blocks were skipped by Hamas and the houses appear ordinary, reminders of how lovely this community was. But, as in all places where terrible things have happened, whether it be Gettysburg, Normandy, Auschwitz, or here, your knowledge of events brings you to feel spirits around you.

After several blocks, we reach the kibbutz recreation area. Nectar points out a community swimming pool.

"You have a pool?" I ask.

She smiles for the first time. Yes—and more. There is also a full-length basketball court covered from the sun by a large awning. They had a petting zoo and a communal dining place.

"You had everything," I say.

"Yes," says Nectar. "Everything."

The kindergarten area is the hardest to see. A window with fractures and a bullet hole catches my attention. To remember, I ask Robby, my guide, to take a picture of me through it.

I walk into the kindergarten's wash-up area, a big space. It's mostly demolished, but the charmingly low sinks for small children are still intact. Standing out among the ruins is a large stuffed dog left on a chair.

It's often the little things at Be'eri that have the greatest impact, like this stuffed children's dog among the ruins of the kindergarten area. (Photo by Mark Patinkin)

In the nearby medical center, I see a poster in a burned-out room of a young woman named Amit Man. "Murdered here," the poster says in English. Amit was 22 years old and a paramedic. She had long brown hair with light tan highlights. Early on, some of the injured made their way to the medical center, and Amit was helping treat them while others tried to barricade the entryways. It went like that for hours, but the militants at last broke in.

I was struck by this poster of Amit Man, 22, placed where she was murdered in the community's health center. Amit treated the day's wounded until Hamas broke in and shot her in the head. (Photo by Mark Patinkin)

When they did, Nectar tells us 14 inside were slaughtered, including Amit. One nurse survived by hiding. Two of the wounded also somehow survived, one of which later said Amit, the paramedic, spent hours tending to him. Many of the dead here and throughout the kibbutz bled to death after being shot—that's how long it took for help to come. Later, the *Times of Israel* quoted Amit's fellow paramedic and friend Oshrit Haddad saying of her, "She continued to help patients under fire. She fought for their lives until the last moments."

Shortly before she was killed, Amit sent a message to her sister Haviva saying she had been shot in the leg. Then she texted: "They're here. They're in the clinic. I don't think I'll make it out of here. Please be strong if something happens to me."

When Israeli soldiers at last regained control of Be'eri, Amit's body was found with a tourniquet on her left leg and a gunshot wound to the head.

As we move on from the clinic, we pass several other tours, one a group from a New York temple wearing bulletproof vests. During the hour we are here, Nectar tells us we had seen only part of the community. The attack was too vast to be able to see it all.

As our tour reaches its end, I ask Nectar where she and her husband are living now.

With a family in Tel Aviv.

Does she have hobbies?

Yes—yoga and jogging. She's studying computer game design and her LinkedIn says she is skilled at Adobe Creative Cloud software. Her favorite game is Fortnite. Ironically, it's a game about surviving attackers.

I ask what she loves most about Be'eri.

"Everything," she says.

Does she plan to come back?

"It's my hope."

When does she think that will be?

She pauses.

"One day," she finally says.

And then she says it again.

Aboud Ashhab brought me to Succariya, a Ramallah coffee house where he loved spending time with his close childhood friend and Brown University classmate, Hisham Awartani, who was shot with two West Bank pals in Burlington, VT. while wearing keffiyehs. (Photo by Mark Patinkin)

EIGHT

RAMALLAH

When I told Israelis I was heading to Ramallah, the hub of the West Bank, some advised I avoid the Palestinian bus. Take a cab, they said. But I wanted to experience basic travel there during a time of restrictions, so I walked to the hardscrabble transit depot by the Damascus Gate in East Jerusalem.

It's a sprawling outdoor area with buses backing into boarding bays. It takes me a while to get my bearings, but I at last zero in on the "218." After a 20-minute wait, it arrives and I step aboard, paying with my green smart card that just about everyone in Israel uses for trains, light rail and buses.

Ramallah is eight miles from Jerusalem, but I've heard the trip now takes over an hour, with a checkpoint halfway and all roads but one closed to a metro area of almost 300,000. Security.

I settle into a seat, the only non-Palestinian among 40 or so aboard. But all feels fine. The bus is modern and comfortable. There was no reason to caution me.

I've been looking forward to this trip since arriving in Israel. I'm on my way to see Hisham Awartani's world.

Hisham grew up in Ramallah and was one of the three Palestinian college students shot on Nov. 25, 2023, in Burlington, Vermont, for the crime of speaking Arabic and wearing black and white keffiyehs while walking.

The three were visiting Hisham's American uncle and grandmother for Thanksgiving. It brought the conflict's echoes to my own neighborhood in Providence, where Hisham, now paralyzed from the waist down, was a junior at Brown University.

I had emailed his mom, Elizabeth Price, asking about visiting her or other family of Hisham's in Ramallah. Elizabeth's father was an American international banker. She was born in Ireland, studied anthropology at Harvard and in 1991, met a gentleman named Ali Awartani while doing research in Ramallah. As she would later put it, "I fell in love with Palestine." And also, despite her family's skepticism, with Ali.

After seven years together, they married and settled in Ramallah. Elizabeth is now a consultant for nonprofits while Ali works in agriculture. Hisham is the oldest of their three kids, his brother age 13, and sister 17.

Elizabeth messaged that she would not be able to meet me in Ramallah since she was now in America with Hisham as he recovered at a Massachusetts rehabilitation hospital. She suggested I instead connect with one of her son's best friends, Aboud Ashhab. He and Hisham, both 21, had shared both a West Bank childhood and the last three years at Brown University.

When I reached out to Aboud, he texted that he was honored I would make the effort to see him in his West Bank hometown, where he was back for semester break. But he was cautious, too, aware that journalists have not always been kind to Palestinians.

Yet he loves Hisham and the two of them see the importance of showing the human side of a people too often vilified. Maybe, he hoped, an article about Hisham's Ramallah background would in some small way help soften the hate.

We agreed on a Saturday, and now I'm aboard Bus 218 as it navigates out of East Jerusalem deeper into the West Bank. Beyond the window, it's urban sprawl the whole way in the classic style of the Jerusalem metro area—light stone buildings crowded together. As we near the Kalandia checkpoint, the road fans out into a half-dozen approach lanes with vehicles so backed up that street vendors are able to walk among us selling wares.

Once we get through, it's another crawl for the next few miles on Ramallah Street, folks getting on and off at various stops, the bus full enough that almost all of us are sharing seats. Finally, we're here, at another outdoor depot packed with buses and pick-up vans.

I step off, use a maps app to get my bearings, and walk a few blocks to Ramallah's center, where I find a lively vibe. The streets are packed, humming with far more buzz than Bethlehem. Crowds squeeze by sidewalk vendors and shops, some of them upscale. I spot a familiar coffee place with a similar logo called "Stars and Bucks." But the war is here, too, with a billboard-size display showing the faces of 60 children killed in Gaza. "We are not numbers," it says.

I text Aboud that I'm here, and he tells me a spot to meet him near the downtown's central circle. As I wait with notebook in hand watching hundreds of passersby, a classy gentleman approaches and asks if I'm a journalist. Guilty. His name is Amad Omar, and it turns out he spent a few decades as a jewelry store guy in Chicago, where I grew up. His shop was on a fashionable street in The Loop. But he came back in 1998 because Ramallah is home.

Amad Omar noticed my reporter's notebook and approached me in downtown Ramallah. He grew up there, spent years as a jeweler in Chicago, but came back to live on the West Bank because it's home. (Photo by Mark Patinkin)

I tell him I like how lively his city is, and, yes, he says, it's a wonderful place, except when "something happens." Like now, with the border sealed and jobs lost. But I came on a good day—on others, stores are shuttered due to strikes called against the Israeli crackdown. Yet today's crowds, says Amad, show that Palestinians, even during times of adversity, know how to keep living. I think to myself—just like the Israelis.

Aboud soon arrives, a polite dark-haired young man in a black turtleneck who can't wait to show me Ramallah. I repeat to him what I'd said to Amad—I love how alive it is here. Aboud shakes his head. It used to be much more. The war and Israeli crackdown, he says, have hurt the economy. Ramallah is the center of the Palestinian Authority—the Washington D.C. of the West Bank with many government agencies—but that means withheld tax remittances have hit thousands of salaries, as have revoked Israel work permits. Some of these sidewalk vendors, Aboud tells me, are skilled tradesmen who, barred from their day jobs across the border, are now selling vegetables and barely making it. Things in Ramallah are hard.

But Aboud is proud of his city.

He has twin 18-year-old brothers who are also about to go Ivy, one at UPenn, the other at Brown, quite a trajectory for young men from the West Bank. Like Hisham and Aboud, they attended the remarkable Ramallah Friends School, a Quaker institution unrivaled here, where kids learn and dream and rise.

As the two of us walk, we pass flavorful coffee and lunch places. Some have a great item I hadn't seen before—shawarma meat towers the size of your thigh on a vertical spit, vendors shaving off slices for pita sandwiches. I'm tempted, but we keep going—Aboud wants me to see a favorite place where he and Hisham would talk and play cards as they planned their young lives.

Earlier, when I told people in America I was heading to the West Bank, most said the same two words: stay safe. They didn't need to. I haven't seen another non-Arab face in the thousands we've walked by, but I feel zero threat—less than in many American neighborhoods. On the other hand, you want to be on your toes as a pedestrian since cars speed within inches of you on the narrow streets. It at times makes me tense, but Aboud doesn't even notice.

We sit for tea and coffee where Aboud and Hisham sat for the same. It's a second-floor café called Succariya with a balcony and Arabesque feel.

I ask about his friend Hisham's shooting. There's no question in Aboud's mind it happened because Arabs are dehumanized—seen as backward, intolerant, and a threat. But he says it's a false stereotype, and he's of course right—I'm struck by the variety around me. As an example, some women here wear hijabs, but many don't, and no one seems to mind. There are plenty of churches, too.

"We went to school with Palestinian Christians," says Aboud. "We're not a Muslim monolith; we're a diverse group of people."

I found Ramallah—considered the West Bank's capital—a welcoming, lively city, despite the hardships of the current Israeli crackdown. (Photo by Joel Carillet)

He likes his coffee the strong Arabic way. It reminds him of how Hisham used to make it in the Brown University dorm where they were roommates.

I ask him to tell more about what Palestinians face.

"There's no civil law for Palestinians," Aboud says. Even those arrested for speeding go to Israeli military tribunals, and thousands are held without trial for reasons not always shared. Because of the need for permits to leave the West Bank, it has never been easy for Aboud to see his aunt and cousins who live in Jerusalem.

"Now it's impossible," he says. Meaning since Oct. 7.

And he tells me the Israeli crackdown has been brutal. Hundreds on the West Bank have been killed in raids, checkpoints, and run-ins with Israeli soldiers, including a 17-year-old Palestinian American from Louisiana named Tawfiq Ajaq the day I was there. He was shot during an encounter with a Jewish settler and an off-duty soldier.

Aboud tells me the incident hit him hard—Tawfiq was an innocent U.S. student here with family to explore his culture. Aboud feels it could have been him. In fact, he says, the previous week, while driving, he suddenly saw an Israeli checkpoint at a random place he didn't expect.

"Had I not hit the brakes early," Aboud says, "I might have been shot." He pauses. "I would have been shot."

I tell him that despite all he's faced, he doesn't seem angry, and it's true; Aboud is a mild-mannered young man.

Palestinians, he says, hear that a lot, and though he knows I meant it as a compliment, he feels it's a form of fearmongering, as if it's a surprise that he's courteous rather than militant. It's a false impression, he tells me, to assume that any Arab who talks about oppression is a radical.

Even Aboud's gastroenterologist dad was arrested decades ago as a student while protesting the occupation and was held for six months in an Israeli jail.

"It's a never-ending story," Aboud says. All West Bank parents, including his and Hisham's, worry about their kids being unfairly targeted.

"It's why they wanted us to study in America. For a safe education."

He pauses.

"Of course, that flipped on its head when Hisham was shot."

It happened around 6:30 p.m. the Saturday after Thanksgiving 2023 while Hisham was walking in Burlington, Vermont with two childhood pals, Kinnan Abdalhamid and Tahseen Ahmad. Growing up, the three had attended the Ramallah Friends School together, as had Aboud, and were thrilled to be accepted to American colleges. Hisham was at Brown, Tahseen at Trinity in Hartford, and Kinnan at Haverford outside Philadelphia.

Because of tensions from the Gaza war and increased settler violence against Palestinians on the West Bank, their parents thought it safer for the boys to stay in America for the Thanksgiving holiday instead of coming home.

All three chose to spend the week with Hisham's grandmother and his Uncle Rich Price, who live in side-by-side houses in Burlington. Hisham had spent summers there and considers the city a second home.

Rich, brother of Hisham's mom Elizabeth, is a guitarist, songwriter and performer who had contracts with both RCA and Geffen Records for his folk-rock band, The Sweet Remains, which opened for artists including Ziggy Marley and Ray LaMontagne. But settling down as a dad of five sons became more important. So he moved to Vermont with his wife, Kimberly, a designer, and began a career in marketing. It was a bit of a homecoming—Rich went to Vermont's Middlebury college, as did I, another connection for me to this tragedy.

On the afternoon of the shooting, Rich's twin 8-year-olds were having a birthday party at a Burlington bowling alley, which you'd think college students wouldn't bother with. But Hisham and his two buddies wanted to support his young cousins.

So they went, got home around 6:15 p.m., then headed out for a stroll fifteen minutes later. They walked the same route they had taken previous nights, past an apartment house on North Prospect Street where a man named Jason Eaton, 48, was living. He'd recently moved to Burlington from Syracuse, New York. His past jobs, often short-term, included farm manager, driver, and maintenance person. News reports have quoted his mother as saying he had life struggles. He also had described himself on X as a "radical citizen pa-trolling demockracy and crapitalism for oathcreepers."

With no provocation, Eaton stepped off the porch and shot the three young men at close range. Kinnan was struck in the gluteal muscle and Tahseen in the chest. As Tahseen fell to the ground, he broke several ribs.

The bullet that struck Hisham lodged in his second thoracic vertebra, a few inches below the neck. He collapsed onto a lawn.

Eaton was later arrested and faces three charges of attempted murder.

Soon after the paramedics arrived, despite his terrible wound, Hisham was able to call his grandmother. There was blood on the screen of his phone.

"Granny," he said, "I've been shot."

She and his Uncle Rich rushed together to the hospital, just blocks from where they live. They were taken to the ER. It was a busy moment, with Hisham tended to by trauma doctors, nurses, and neurologists.

The staff explained the situation to Rich. The bullet had grazed Hisham's left thumb and gone through his clavicle, lodging in his spine.

Despite the situation, Hisham seemed collected.

Hisham Awartani of Ramallah is shown here on a past New England trip with his mother, Elizabeth Price, and his dad Ali Awartani. His uncle Rich Price, of Burlington, provided this photo.

"Hi, Uncle Richard," he said.

"Hisham," said Rich, "I am so sorry this happened to you."

Rich was devastated but impressed by how composed his nephew appeared.

"Hisham has a remarkably unflappable way about him," Rich told me.

Rich would soon learn that the alleged gunman lived nearby and had likely seen the three young men on walks the previous two nights.

"He shot them from six feet away," Rich said. "The fact that Hisham and his friends are still alive, frankly, it's a miracle."

Rich feels the incident shows the danger of Islamophobic rhetoric that paints all Palestinians as extremists.

"I think it's a reflection of the level of vitriol and hate that exists in this country," he told me.

Talking to Rich makes you realize that Hisham is part of an extraordinary family with shared American roots and global ties. Hisham himself has triple citizenship—U.S., Palestinian and Irish.

Of course, Rich Price has been to Ramallah to visit his sister's family. I asked him what life is like there.

"It's an interesting place of stark dichotomy," he told me. "On the one hand, it's a really loving community, a place of warmth and safety in the sense no one locks their doors—very communal. But it's also a place where people are living under military occupation."

Rich describes the situation there with studious calm, devoid of stridency.

"What is difficult for most Americans to visualize about Palestine," he said, "is there really is no autonomous state there. It's completely controlled by Israel. Even the Palestinian Authority is very much beholden and controlled by Israel."

Driving around the West Bank, he said, involves going through many Israeli military checkpoints.

And there is the matter of Jewish settlements.

"The proliferation of illegal settlements," Rich said, "I think would be shocking to most Americans. The slow annexation of the West Bank territory that was once envisioned to be part of a future state of Palestine has become like Swiss cheese—just holes in that land."

Palestinian territory is so encroached upon that Rich says many there are losing hope of a two-state solution. But despite that, his sister Elizabeth's family still embraces living there, finding it a beautiful culture and Ramallah a sophisticated city.

"Palestine," said Rich, "has one of the highest percentages of PhDs. They say there that education is an act of resistance."

His nephew Hisham reflects that.

"He's deeply committed to his studies," said Rich. Impressively, Hisham speaks seven languages including English, Arabic, German and Italian. At Brown, he's a dual major—math and archeology.

"And he's very kind," Rich said, "quite thoughtful. A good cousin to my boys."

When I talked to Rich in mid-December, three weeks after the shooting, he told me Hisham was showing remarkable resilience.

"He's really thrown himself into the work of his recovery," said Rich. "He's engaged, asking questions and advocating on behalf of himself."

Although there is hope for improvement, Rich says the prognosis remains difficult.

"But there are two components to a recovery like this," he told me. "One is medical, and the second is mindset and spirit and attitude. And Hisham is bringing his best self to that challenge."

The war has made travel from the West Bank difficult, and Hisham's parents weren't able to make it to Burlington until four days after the shooting. During that time, Rich and his mom took turns sitting vigil at Hisham's bedside in the hospital ICU, sometimes past 3 a.m., with equipment beeping and nurses coming in and out to check vitals.

Hisham was in an area next to his two friends, who were being treated, too. Rich was there for many poignant moments as the three young men, fighting both pain and the trauma of what had happened, got each other through.

At one point, one of the three said to the others: "I just want to ask the guy, 'Why?'"

During the hospital vigils, Rich at times thought back to when all were gathered around the Thanksgiving table just days before talking about what they were thankful for. When it was Hisham's turn, he smiled and said, "Pumpkin pie with vanilla ice cream."

More than once, when Rich got back home from the hospital, the anguish about his nephew left him briefly sobbing, something his wife hadn't seen him do in 18 years of marriage.

Rich Price at the family's 2023 Thanksgiving dinner in Burlington with his nephew Hisham, on the table's right, and Hisham's Ramallah friends Kinnan Abdalhamid and Tahseen Ahmad on the left. All three young men were shot two days later. (Photo courtesy of Rich Price).

"It's devastating to see someone who was working so hard to build a meaningful, bright future have this setback," he told me.

But ironically, it was Hisham's grace, even after being told he would likely be a paraplegic, that comforted Rich.

"He was approaching this challenge with a level of bravery I don't think I could have mustered at age 21," Rich said. Or even now.

Rich feels it comes both from Hisham's mature nature, and the life he lived.

"It's difficult to be a young Palestinian man in this world," said Rich. "It requires resilience, it requires fortitude—the ability to persevere in the face of great hardships."

In Hisham's case, said Rich, there is also a great sense of humor. In a statement read to a gathered vigil for him at Brown on Nov. 27, Hisham wrote, "Who knew that all I had to do to become famous was to get shot?"

But he added more seriously: "Your mind should not just be focused on me as an individual, but rather as a proud member of the people being oppressed."

Months later, in an op-ed in *The New York Times*, Hisham wrote of the same dehumanization that Aboud had been telling me about.

"This system of othering—Israeli-only roads, fenced-off settlements, the 'security' wall—is an inherent part of the Israeli state psyche," Hisham wrote. "Yet far from ensuring Israelis' safety, it instead inflicts mass humiliation on Palestinians."

Hisham wrote that he looked forward to coming home to Ramallah. But he added something will happen when he returns to the West Bank.

"I (will) cease to be a junior at Brown University," he wrote, "a student of archaeology and mathematics, a San Francisco Giants fan, a Balkan history nerd. My entire identity will be reduced to my capacity for violence, not as a human being, but as a Palestinian."

Once Hisham's parents were able to be with him at the rehab

facility near Boston, Rich began mostly checking in by phone from Burlington. During one call, Hisham told his uncle he's embarrassed that so much fuss has been made about him, given how many thousands have died in Gaza.

"He looked at the list of the dead in Gaza," Rich recalled, "and noticed there were about 30 Hishams—and Hisham is not a super common name in Palestine. And he said, 'I'm the Hisham people know, but there are at least 30 Hishams people don't know.'"

Hisham's grace has left Rich wondering if there's a greater plan.

"It's rare in this country for Palestinians to be portrayed in humanizing, positive ways," he says. "The silver lining is the way he and his friends are providing a human face as to what it means to be Palestinians—that they're a people of great love, intelligence and compassion."

Rich is convinced this is just the beginning, and Hisham will have an impact on the world.

And now here in Ramallah, at Succariya, Aboud and I are finishing our coffee and tea. We head outside and walk to his and Hisham's favorite lunch spot, Abu Johnny, a barbecue grill with sidewalk seating.

As we settle at a table, I ask how Hisham is doing in rehab back in the States. This was in January, two months after the shooting.

"I talked to him a few days ago," says Aboud. "He's hoping to come back to Brown and start the spring semester."

I ask why the two of them love Ramallah and the West Bank so much.

For one thing, Aboud says, it's more social than America—you start the day with no plans and end up hanging with 10 or 12 friends. Then he observes an amusing difference. The West Bank has cleaner, um, facilities. Aboud and Hisham are still freaked out by how gross America's public bathrooms are.

Soon, they bring us our dishes, big ones, of spicy chicken and lamb kebabs, with hummus, vegetables and hot shatta sauce. I am learning there is no such thing as small portions with Palestinians.

How, I ask, are Hisham's spirits holding up?

His physical therapy is going well, and he's recovering mentally. Indeed, most of Hisham's public statements have not been about himself. Even when it's just the two of them talking, Hisham tells Aboud he's better off than people in Gaza, where some have limbs amputated without anesthesia because there isn't any. Hisham wants the focus there.

Where, I ask, does Hisham's strength come from?

Aboud answers with the Arabic word "sumud." It means steadfastness, which Palestinians get from what they've been through.

"Overcoming adversity?" I ask.

Aboud says that word is too general, even cliché, and misses Palestinian truth.

"It's overcoming oppression and violence," he says.

He adds: "People have lost family, land and houses—but not the pride in who they are."

Finally, it's time for me to head back. On our way to the bus pickup, we pass their favorite ice cream parlor, called Rukab's.

"Me and Hisham love this place," says Aboud. "It's the best ice cream in Palestine."

Aboud likes the dark chocolate, Hisham pistachio. The shop opened in Ramallah in 1941. Their ice-cream, beloved among Palestinians, is known for its stretchy texture. The two wish they had a Rukab's near Brown.

Aboud tells me he will be heading back to school in America soon but needs to leave Ramallah three days early to navigate the sometimes-difficult Jordan border, controlled by Israel, to the airport in Amman. Like most West Bank Palestinians, he's not allowed to fly out of nearby Ben Gurion near Tel Aviv.

As we walk, Aboud takes me to the gate of the Ramallah Friends School, which teaches 1,600 students from kindergarten through 12th grade on two campuses. This is its main one, a spacious island near the crowded heart of the city. Aboud says he and Hisham still treasure their days there. And treasure Ramallah, too. He says it's a part of their Palestinian souls.

We say goodbye and I'm again struck by how safe I felt in Ramallah, and how rich a culture it is.

It's almost dusk when my bus back to Jerusalem gets to the Kalandia checkpoint. This time, it's not a step-off-and-on situation. I have to exit, show my passport, go through a metal detector, then walk 100 yards to another outdoor depot. I wait there a half hour for the Jerusalem bus as darkness comes down.

Although I saw no other non-Palestinian faces the day I was in Ramallah, I never felt uncomfortable there.

Finally, I arrive back at the Damascus Gate bus depot, walking past the Old City and then another 20 minutes up Jaffa Street to my hotel.

Later that night, Aboud is nice enough to check in on me by WhatsApp.

He's happy I'm back in Jerusalem.

He never mentions that despite his Ivy pedigree, and aunt and cousins living here, that as a Palestinian man, it's a place he's not allowed to go.

He thanks me for having come to see his world, and Hisham's.

I tell him I was honored that he shared it.

And understand why they're so proud of it.

In Hostage Square in Tel Aviv, I approached Itzik Horn to ask if he knew the two hostages whose faces were on his shirt. Yes, he said, they are his sons, both still missing. (Photo by Mark Patinkin)

NINE

HOSTAGE SQUARE

The image to me is a symbol of Oct. 7—a young woman named Naama Levy dragged by Hamas men into a car, bleeding between her legs, her hands zip-tied and ankles slashed.

It's why I reached out to speak with her mother, Ayelet, and at first, she said yes. As with many hostage parents, there is the hope that each bit of publicity might help. But as the day approached, Ayelet sent a message of apology; she was emotionally spent and needed time apart. Often, when someone can't speak about a thing, it says more than if they could.

It happened again with two other families of the kidnapped. I at first got a yes, but shortly before our interview, they decided they couldn't do it. The toll of 100 days had drained them.

And so I went to Hostage Square.

It's the now-famous plaza in the heart of Tel Aviv where, once or more a week, thousands gather asking for the missing to be brought home.

This was such a day—a huge crowd drawn there for a poignant milestone. A hostage was marking an important birthday in captivity. His name is Kfir Bibas. It is his first birthday. He is the youngest of the taken. He had been gone a third of his life. As I write this, it's over half.

Speakers on a stage are addressing the crowd in Hebrew. I do not understand the words, but I don't need to. More than one begins to weep and has to pause.

I walk to the back of the crowd, and, after a few minutes, randomly approach a 70-ish couple named Mickey and Ronit. They do not know any hostages personally but come here once a week as their way of saying the kidnapped are remembered. A few days before, a group had gathered at the Gaza border with megaphones to shout "You're not alone" across the fence. Of course, it was impossible that any hostages could hear them, but that is how people in Israel are coping with this.

In one part of the square is a mock Hamas tunnel made of gray fiberglass that takes you minutes to walk through. Inside it, you hear the sound of explosions from loudspeakers. It's lit by occasional bare bulbs. Messages to the missing are written on its walls.

Speakers onstage continue to give their stories. Although there are thousands here, many holding signs, it's less a protest than a vigil. As you walk among the crowd, you realize their cause is why the war goes on. It is, of course, about Hamas, but even more, about the missing, Israel being as much a family as a country.

I spot an older gentleman in a black T-shirt printed with the faces of two of the missing. They are both young men; at least you hope the word "are" is still true. But you don't know. Nobody here does.

I ask the man if he has connections with the two faces on the shirt.

I lingered by a now famous empty table in Hostage Square, set with bottles of dirty water and moldy bread, a reminder of the missing, and their conditions. (Photo by Mark Patinkin)

Yes. He knows them well—they are his sons.

We are standing by a long table with more than 100 empty chairs. There is a place-setting in front of each, many with unclean water in glasses and old bread on plates to reflect the conditions of the kidnapped. Some of the chairs are wrapped in barbed wire. There are red paper butterflies near each of the settings, and the symbolism is clear. If only.

The father in the T-shirt is named Itzik Horn, pronounced like Isaac. His boys are Iair, 45, and Eitan, 37. They were taken into Gaza from a kibbutz called Nir Oz. Forty-six people were slaughtered there. Scores were kidnapped, Itzik's boys among them.

I ask Itzik how he is doing.

In accented English, he simply says the word "impossible."

In late November, some of the 50 who were freed in the first hostage release said they had seen Itzik's sons, and they didn't seem to be wounded. That's Itzik's only solace. But no one knows what's happened in the months since then.

Talking about it seems painful to him. I ask if he's been able to sleep. Itzik gives a look as if to say I should know the answer to that question. Indeed, his face is lined in a way that has to do with things other than his 71 years.

Itzik is now retired from his work as a teacher and principal. I ask what his boys are like.

Both are still single, he says, and they love watching soccer. Both were strong supporters of Palestinian rights. Most of the massacred were the same. Hamas, Itzik says, targeted the people who were for peace.

Iair, the older brother, was in construction and helped run the pub at kibbutz Nir Oz. Eitan worked with youth groups where he lived north of Tel Aviv. He's also a singer and songwriter. He was visiting his brother when it happened.

I ask Itzik if there is a message he wants to give.

Only to ask the American government to try to do … something.

I ask if there is a moment or story about his boys that reflects who they are. At that, he gets visibly emotional, then apologizes and walks on, unable to talk of it any longer.

As I move through the crowd, I spot a man in a wheelchair who gives his name as Doron Zexer, 50. He is wearing a black T-shirt with the face of a young man over words in Hebrew that say, "Bring Edan home now."

The young man's full name is Edan Alexander. He grew up in Tenafly, New Jersey, and moved to Israel in 2022 after high school with a cultural immersion program. Doron was his host father. Edan decided to stay on, recently joining the Israel Defense Forces instead of returning to the states to go to college.

He's now among the kidnapped. They took him at age 19 and he has since turned 20. Edan, said Doron, had just started a new love with a fellow soldier named Shira.

Doron looks upon Edan like a son, but he said he has a heart for every hostage, which is why he is here, and often is.

"If Edan came home tomorrow," says Doron, "I would still come here every day until the last one comes home."

I am about to leave when I see a man wearing an orange T-shirt that says, "Free My Family Now." The shirt has a drawing of a family of four. The man is also wearing a metal dog tag that says, "My heart was kidnapped in Gaza."

His name is Eli Bibas, and it turns out he's the grandfather of Kfir, the youngest hostage whose first birthday is being celebrated by these thousands. As a reporter, I might have wanted to talk to Kfir's parents, Yarden, 34, and Shiri, 32, but I can't. They were kidnapped, too. So was their other child, 4-year-old Ariel. The whole family is still gone. A drawing of all of them is on Eli's shirt.

There is difficult video of the young family being taken, including CCTV footage of militants drilling open the door of the Bibas home in Kibbutz Nir Oz around 9:45 a.m. Shortly afterward, Yarden texted his sister saying, "They're in."

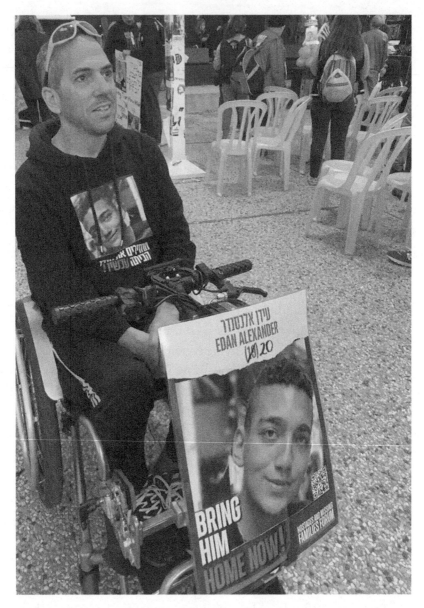

At Hostage Square, I ran into Doron Zexer, the Israeli host dad to Edan Alexander, 20, of Tenafly, N.J., who, after a cultural immersion program, decided to join the IDF, and was kidnapped into Gaza only months later by Hamas on Oct. 7. (Photo by Mark Patinkin)

Later on Oct. 7, a now infamous video was posted by Hamas of Shiri looking terrified while holding onto her young children with militants around her. Shiri's parents, Yosi and Margit Silberman, both Nir Oz residents, were murdered in the attack. Shiri's father, who worked in the kibbutz auto shop, was 67 and her mother, an education staffer, was 63.

Months later, another video surfaced of Yarden, the father, inside Gaza on the day of the attack. He had been forced onto a motorcycle, and is surrounded by scores of yelling men in a chaotic street scene. The motorcycle's driver, sitting in front of Yarden, waves a handgun while others around them hold up rifles. Another man wedges behind Yarden. The mob seems to be civilians, most with guns, a sign of how heavily armed the people are in Gaza. At various times, some of the men put Yarden into a headlock with their arms. He holds up his hands as if to ask, "Why?" The out-of-control yelling never stops. At one point in the footage, there is blood on Yarden's face, a sign he was being struck even as the video was taken. He seems to cower as men swarm him. At another point, he covers his head to avoid being beaten. There is blood on his hands, too.

Yarden worked as a welder while his wife Shiri was a childminder and accountant. They lived in a small kibbutz house with a tire swing. The two had discussed moving because of rocket attacks and being so close to Gaza. At age 4 and age 1, their children are the youngest hostages. The next-youngest is 18. It is a mystery why Hamas would keep a baby and a young child. Or maybe it isn't.

Eli, the grandfather I am now speaking with here in Hostage Square, is retired from a career as an air-conditioning tech. I ask him if it has gotten any easier after these three-plus months.

If anything, he says, it's harder. With the focus now on Gaza casualties, he worries the world is forgetting the hostages, or doesn't care about them because they are Jews.

I saw Eli Bibas by a clock in Hostage Square showing 103 days had passed since his son Yarden, daughter-in-law Shiri and their two children, Ariel, 4, and Bibas, age 1, were taken hostage. The day I took this picture was Bibas's first birthday. (Photo by Mark Patinkin)

Behind him is a huge digital clock marking how long the hostages have been in captivity. The reading on it is 103 days, 10 hours, 20 minutes and 37 seconds.

You stand there and look as it continues the count—38 seconds, 39—and you wonder if it will reach another 100 days before this is over, or even 1,000.

For a brief moment, the grandfather of the youngest hostage glances at the clock.

Then he and other family members walk off and are soon lost in the crowd.

In 1991, when the Israelis occupied Gaza, I went on a Jeep patrol commanded by Oded Turbahn, then 34, who got out at one point to survey the Jabalia refugee camp. Our Jeep that day was hit by hundreds of stones thrown by kids and teens. (Photo by Mark Patinkin)

TEN

ON JEEP PATROL DURING
THE INTIFADA

I am at my desk in Providence working on this book when an unexpected email arrives.

During that 1991 trip of mine, a time Israel still occupied Gaza, I'd spent a day on patrol there in an IDF Jeep. The commander behind the wheel was Oded Turbahn, 34 back then. I hadn't been in touch with him in the decades since, but out of the blue, in March 2024, the fifth month of the Hamas war, Oded sent me a message.

He was now 68. One of his grandkids had done a deep Google search of him and came across the 1991 article I'd done.

"It is my first time reading it," he wrote.

Oded had been in tech as a businessman, more recently running a factory in Israel for the Los Angeles-based Dollar Shave Club, retiring a few years ago.

He added something revealing.

"I am surprised and sad," said Oded, "that nothing has changed."

He meant in Gaza even before the Oct. 7 war.

"It was a similar situation to what I showed you in 1991," Oded wrote.

The difference, he added, is that it had gone from the stone-throwing I witnessed to missiles. And now war.

We set up a time to talk. Meanwhile, 33 years later, I still remember those stones bouncing off Oded Turbahn's IDF Jeep as we drove on patrol through the streets of the Gaza Strip.

»» ««

I arrived that day in November 1991 at Israel's main Gaza outpost just outside the territory's entry checkpoint, after a two-hour drive from Jerusalem. The sun was warm as loud traffic went by on a nearby civilian roadway—the one that would later be at the heart of the Oct. 7 slaughter. The IDF base was mostly tents and Army-green vehicles. Soldiers sat at faded picnic tables holding American M-16s and short-stock Israeli automatic Galils.

The officer in charge, tall and lean with dark hair, introduced himself as Oded Turbahn. He was on reserve duty—most Israeli men do a month or more a year up to age 55. Because he was a commander, Oded did up to three months. Normally, he was chief of a tank battalion, but tanks weren't used in civilian patrol. At least at that time. The need for them during the Gaza occupation would come later.

As we walked toward the Jeep, I asked about Oded's regular job. He was a local product manager for a Pennsylvania-based company making semiconductor equipment. He spoke of how much he loved going to the States. He had three children, 8, 5 and 1.

"How do you feel about this duty?" I asked.

"I don't like it," he said. "But I like my country."

I climbed into the cramped, messy back of the Jeep. There were dusty riot helmets by my head, and on the floor, the tools of occupation during an intifada—tear gas projectiles, rubber bullets, and shock grenades.

The Jeep's windows, which had gun portholes, were hard plastic and covered with tight chain-link. Because of Molotov cocktails, the vehicle was also fire-resistant.

Another soldier sat opposite me, Jacob, a 40-year-old lawyer. The intifada had gone for three years, but lately, there were only a few confrontations a day. Jacob told me that counted as a lull.

"I don't know," he said, "I guess they're tired." There's a chance, he predicted, that there would be no incidents this afternoon. At that, a voice crackled over the radio about a Jewish settler in Gaza who just got attacked by stone throwers.

Jacob smiled.

"Like I was saying."

>»» «« <

We took off as the lead Jeep in a three-vehicle convoy. After only five minutes or so, we pulled off the road by a briefing tent, where Oded went over our planned route on a wall map. He said we might stay outside the refugee camps today; such places can be combustible—but he would decide that later. He told me you have to find a balance—if you start avoiding such places, extremists get bolder.

I asked if they are often hit with stones on patrol. He shared a smile with the other soldiers.

"Of course," he said. "In certain areas, it's almost every child. It doesn't matter what his age, 4 or 5 years old. I can't understand it."

He recalled a week before when hundreds began pelting two soldiers on foot. "Big rocks," Oded said. "They were trying to kill them. They wouldn't stop. So the soldiers shot at their legs, and they still wouldn't stop. I can't understand."

Do they get hit with many Molotov cocktails?

Two or three a week.

His was one of the few rifles with a scope. Oded explained that only he and his chief deputy can decide to use live ammunition, unless a soldier is in danger of being killed.

Some Palestinians describe Israelis as surly, even brutal, so I asked if this duty—daily stonings—hardens soldiers?

The older reservists have good restraint, Oded said. The 20-year-olds take the stones more personally, so it's important for a commander to keep talking to them.

As we headed back to the Jeep, another reserve soldier, a 40ish man named Steve, walked beside me and began chatting. He was soft-poken, serious, a television editor in civilian life who immigrated from Britain 20 years before. Now he was on his own one-month tour patrolling Gaza. His tone hinted that I'd touched on something he had been struggling with.

Controlling anger, he said, is the hardest part of this duty.

"You're open to so much insult," he told me, "just incredible bottle throwing and rock throwing. The provocation is immense."

"Don't they back off when you respond?"

"It's almost the opposite," he said. "They want you to fight back. They want you to hate them, mistreat them."

Why?

"Because," Steve said, "they know it helps their cause if we look like monsters; it's as if they are saying: arrest me, beat me, shoot me, because if we make you act brutal, the world will see you as occupiers, and that will help us get free."

Does it work?

With some soldiers, he said, they succeed.

As I write this in 2024, it strikes me that Hamas no doubt had the same thinking on Oct. 7, knowing what the IDF would do in response, and how Israel would look in the eyes of countless people around the world.

Did Steve understand why Gazans resented and even hated him?

On one hand, he saw his mission as protecting Palestinians from extremists who want to run Gaza.

"But I personally understand," he said. "They see us as an occupying army. I suppose they feel we're here to repress them."

He had a solemn air about him. Gaza, he said, affected him that way. In earlier tours, the abuse made him angry; now it just leaves him emotionally down.

»» ««

While catching up in 2024, I asked Oded if he had other photos from his Gaza patrol days. He found this one of himself, with an expression reflecting the grimness of the job.

We climbed back inside and took off, Oded, two soldiers and myself, followed by two other Jeeps. At one point on a side street, a soccer ball rolled in front of us. The Jeep stopped, and one of the three got out to toss the ball back to the kids. This, Oded explained, is one of the more sedate areas, where you can have a friendly interaction.

Ten minutes later, we pulled up to a busy intersection by the border, hundreds of Gazans returning on buses from working the day in Israel. Two soldiers stood watch on a curb. I approached one—Joseph, 28, an industrial engineer, married two months ago. I asked his mission.

To guard commuters from extremists, he said. He mentioned a phrase seen from time to time in graffiti here: "If you work in Israel, we will kill you." And yet many need those jobs for a living wage.

We chatted for a moment, and like most soldiers here, Joseph saw his job as protecting civilians who wanted to live here peacefully. The tone was sincere—and common. Israel's Gaza occupation was being conducted by lawyers and product managers wanting only to keep the peace.

But through Palestinian eyes, they were intimidating occupiers—wardens with truncheons and worse.

The irony is that both images were right. There is no one truth in Gaza, just two perceptions.

»» ««

We continued driving, leaving the crowds behind as we steered onto a dirt road along the territory's barbed wire border. There were no buildings here, just fields kept as a buffer for security—the same as today. It's likely we passed some of the spots where, 33 years later, Hamas militants would break through the fence into Israel.

Then we turned back in, stopping by an army observation post overlooking the biggest refugee camp in the territories, Jabalia. Below us was a messy, sprawling slum. We could hear prayers broadcast from mosques. Jabalia, said Oded, was where emotions ran highest and stone-throwing could be the worst.

It was also where the intifada began in December of 1987 when an Israeli truck struck a car, killing four Palestinians. Rumors spread that it was intentional, and soon after, a petrol bomb was thrown at IDF soldiers, triggering riots that spread through Gaza and the West Bank. It turned into a years-long cycle of violent protests, terrorist attacks, and Israeli crackdowns that killed over 1,000 Palestinians and 160 Israelis.

There in Gaza, Oded decided to patrol through Jabalia after all. I was in the lead car with him as we wound our way through streets as narrow as alleyways. We passed chickens, geese, goats, trash. Nearby, I heard a sharp whistle which turned into a hundred whistles.

"It's a sign that we are here," said Oded.

As we paused at an intersection, some kids playing in a vacant lot spotted us. They were young teens and didn't pause to discuss what to do—they simply grabbed stones and began to run after us while flinging them. We were far enough ahead that nothing hit. I waited for the soldiers to pull over and chase them; that's what their television image has been in America. Instead, Oded kept going.

"If I stop," he said, "they will keep throwing, and I don't want them to get hurt. Or us."

Does he ever confront the stone-throwers?

Yes, at times. The people here know each patrol, each Jeep. If you never respond, they become more violent, so at times you must. But it is the hardest decision—when to do so. Take the matter of roadblocks set up to stop the Jeeps, usually made of burning tires. Go around them too often, said Oded, and the streets will soon fill with them. But how do you clear them? If you send your own men to do it, it's often a trap. Another option is to order those living nearby to remove them; but is that fair?

"How would you feel if some soldier knocked on your door and said, 'Move this mess out here?'" he said. "This is the image of the occupier. It's a very unpleasant business."

We kept going, the tires kicking up sandy dust that covered the Jeep and filtered inside. When I closed my teeth, I felt grains of sand.

We turned a corner.

"This is called the surprise road," said Oded. "We are always surprised by stones here."

Up ahead, a group of kids saw us coming. They began to run away, but didn't go far.

"Windows," said Oded. "Doors." I was the nearest one to the plastic swing doors on the back of the Jeep, so I closed them. Faces peered at us as we got close. Nothing yet.

"They're waiting for the last Jeep to go by," Oded said.

He was right—as soon as the convoy passed, several kids leapt out. The third Jeep took hits, but we kept going. Out of fairness, Oded soon pulled over and let the others go to the safer front of the line. Now we were the back Jeep.

Up ahead, on another side street, 20 or so kids were playing, several of them girls. They, too, looked in their early teens, maybe less.

"Get ready," said Oded, "I know this place."

These ones didn't wait for us to start to pass them. As soon as we were alongside, they flung rocks right at us. One projectile startled me, slamming into a side window near my ear. Here on the inside, it was hard to keep from reacting personally. One older boy met my eyes and threw a rock directly at my face. In many situations, said Oded, you can hear them yell things at you. A favorite phrase in Arabic is "Son of a whore."

Once we got ahead of them, they fell in behind us, still throwing. I was sitting opposite a young soldier named Elazar. He was 19. He opened the back doors and lifted his rifle in their direction. From the kids' point of view, it must have looked ominous, a uniformed Israeli soldier in a military vehicle waving the muzzle of an M-16 after being provoked with rocks.

Astonishingly, it had no effect. The kids kept throwing. Several girls threw, too.

"Aren't they scared of anything?" I asked.

"They know we don't shoot them," said Elazar.

The rocks kept coming, and the faces suddenly reminded me of something. This wasn't my first day in Gaza. I'd spent two earlier days seeing things from the Palestinian side, staying in an old Gaza Inn called Marna House with the flavor of a 1940s movie. The proprietress showed me a BBC documentary on Gaza's children of the streets. One of the boys was interviewed about whether he got scared while throwing stones at soldiers. No, he just thinks of a common street chant: "The martyr is God's beloved one." That's the kind of mindset indoctrinated in the Gaza Strip. It is still like that today in 2024.

From the front seat, Oded started counting. "One stone, two, three." Soon, it was almost nonstop. Every 30 seconds or so, another bunch attacked us.

"Look at this," said Oded. "What can you think? They hate us."

Many of the stones sailed wildly. An older Arab man came around the corner and was almost hit. He said nothing to the boys. Not a single adult who saw any of this said anything.

Another rock again hit next to my ear, and I flinched backward. Oded noticed, then wrapped his knuckles against the plastic of his own window.

"Don't worry," he said, "it's good stuff."

We'd been hit by dozens of stones by now, maybe a hundred. I'd lost count. Hundreds more had been thrown.

And then I saw an astonishing sight. A child—he could not have been over 4—ran after the Jeep and flung a stone. I aimed my camera through the dirty plastic window and captured it.

"They learn to throw before they learn to walk," Oded said. "They hate us from birth."

At every turn, we took more stones, but throughout, Oded just kept going. He'd decided not to confront them this time.

I wondered again how I'd think if I were the one being targeted like this every day. My mind went back to a talk I had with a former Israeli officer who did duty in both Gaza and the West Bank.

"We'd have stones thrown at us," he said, "Molotov cocktails hitting our Jeeps. On foot, a mother comes out and hits you. And it's 110 degrees, and some Arab walks by and spits on you. And he'll say your mother's a whore and your sister's a whore, and you have to take it because you're not allowed to cock your gun unless you're threatened. And despite it all, these young soldiers show incredible restraint, but the papers don't write about that. All they write about is the one of 1,000 incidents when a soldier does kill someone, though you never read that he was about to be killed himself."

I soon lost count of how many stones hit our patrol Jeep that day in 1991–there were hundreds, but one moment stood out. A child around 4 or 5 ran behind the vehicle and flung one more rock. I aimed my camera through the dirty plastic window and captured it (Photo by Mark Patinkin).

The ex-officer went on: "After a while, these young soldiers get frustrated and angry, and it's got to show somewhere. I had one soldier at a checkpoint, and an old man came by with a donkey and a cart—filled with watermelons. I heard the soldier say, 'You want to get through, give us five watermelons.' I went up to him and said, 'That's why they hate us—you're becoming like every occupier in the world.' And he almost started crying and said, 'Thank you for keeping me from turning into a monster.' But that's the danger. It's hard for even decent occupiers not to act like occupiers."

I looked over at Elazar, only 19 and just beginning his duty here. He seemed to be without cynicism, and I wondered how long that would last.

In Jerusalem, I had spoken with an Israeli doctor whose son did a tour in the territories.

"The thing we hate them for the most," he said, "is what they've done to our kids. You can only turn your cheek so long. You have 100 people start coming at you with ax handles and knives. You have to defend yourself; you shoot or die. And afterward, something changes in our kids, something moves, and they are never the same again."

He then asked: is the price of being an occupier worth that?

Finally, after a few hours, the patrol was done. We pulled into the army outpost, where my guide and car were waiting. I said goodbye to Oded, and soon, we were at the checkpoint gate where we'd entered the base. A young soldier there approached to ask us how it went. As he was about to wave us through, he spotted my camera and notebook.

He paused to ask whether I was a journalist. When I told him yes, from America, he began talking earnestly. He'd love to study there. And travel there.

"You don't like this assignment?" I asked.

His expression said I of course could not be serious. I looked at his face. He was no more than 20. He was 20 and he was stuck. And it was not the army he minded being stuck in—the army was part of the lives of all Israelis. It was Gaza. He was stuck in Gaza and he did not want to be there.

»» ««

And now it's 2024 and I'm dialing Oded Turbahn's number—the first time we will have spoken since that 1991 Jeep patrol. He tells me he's living outside Tel Aviv with his second wife, having lost his first to cancer 14 years ago. He's 68 but says he was born on Feb. 29, Leap Day, so jokes he's technically 17.

Both of Oded's sons live near San Francisco, one a project manager with a cloud computing firm, the other an MIT grad and co-founder of Dynamic, a crypto startup. Chuckling, Oded says he doesn't understand the company, but it got seed money from the notable venture firm Andreessen Horowitz, so he's okay with it. His daughter is an industrial engineer in Israel.

I tell him his kids seem to have turned out well.

"That's because I never interfered with my first wife raising them," Oded says—it was all her.

I ask if he'd been to Gaza since that 1991 posting.

Yes—he continued to do reserve duty up to 80 days annually, required of Israeli commanders. That paused in 1996 when Oded moved to San Francisco for two years as a product guy for chip equipment maker Applied Materials, helping them transition from 8-inch wafers to the current 12-inch. Most recently, he ran the Dollar Shave Club factory in Israel before retiring.

I ask if his Gaza mission changed in the years after I rode with him.

Yes, his battalion began to spend more time protecting Palestinians who commuted to Israel to work. Increasingly, extremists didn't want them to.

"Similar as you see today with the humanitarian aid," Oded says, "the way Hamas takes control of the food the world is bringing in." Hamas, he says, puts civilians second.

Back then, despite the rock throwing, Oded found some Gazans didn't mind Israelis keeping order. When he talked to folks one-on-one, many whispered that militants were a menace. He feels it was the same in recent years.

"The people just want to have jobs and live a quieter life," Oded tells me.

But by now I'd learned a truth about places like Gaza, as well as

Hezbollah-controlled areas of Lebanon I wrote about in 1987—if 10 percent of a population are extremists with guns, there is little the rest can do about it.

It's a tragedy, Oded tells me, that among other things, Oct. 7 destroyed the chance for Gazans to work in Israel. That was a big part of their economy. But it will be years before they're allowed back in, if ever. Hamas, he says, knew that would happen and didn't care—just as they knew it would start a destructive war. Two million Gazans, says Oded, had their lives ruined for a day of slaughtering Jews.

I ask if the IDF has gone overboard—did there have to be so much destruction of Gaza buildings?

"Unfortunately, Israel was forced to find a way to protect itself," he says. Because Hamas fights in and under schools, mosques, and homes, there was no choice but to target them there. History, he says, has shown that starting a war against a strong army can be catastrophic for the attackers. Look at what happened to Germany and Japan in World War II. And the same in many other conflicts. That is forgotten, he says, in the way Israel is now being judged.

In the years after I was there in 1991, Oded saw the militancy in Gaza increase.

"When you met me," says Oded, "they just threw stones. But then they started to shoot guns and missiles."

At that point, the Israelis brought in armor, including tanks.

"You'd be killed right away in Jeeps," Oded says.

During his 1990s service in the strip, 8,000 Jews were living in 21 Gazan settlements. His soldiers often escorted them back home from trips outside. That stopped in 2005, when Israel ended the occupation, ordering the settlers to leave. Many refused and had to be forced out—in some cases literally dragged away by fellow Jews in the IDF.

But Oded was in favor of it. He has long been on the left, believing in a Palestinian state. He hoped a Gaza that was free of Jewish patrols—and Jews—would be a promising experiment in

Palestinian self-determination. Despite the poverty there, Oded saw its potential. If Gaza's 25-mile Mediterranean beach were developed more, it could draw tourists, maybe even Israelis one day. A flourishing, peaceful Gaza, Oded hoped, could be a model for Israeli-Palestinian coexistence.

Back in the 1990s, Oded used to debate that with a fellow soldier named Yossi, a hardliner who was among the Gazan settlers in his regular life. Sometimes, as the two went on patrol, Oded would tell him that if Israel withdrew, they'd have peace.

"If we have real peace," Yossi responded, "I'll give up my house." He would pay that price. But the Palestinians, Yossi said, wanted Jews driven from Israel itself, not just Gaza.

Oded tried to insist that the two sides could coexist as neighbors.

Yossi pushed back. If the occupation ended, he'd say, Gaza would soon be run by extremists plotting attacks on Israel.

"We have no one to negotiate with," Yossi told Oded. "They just want to kill us."

Oded and Yossi are still friends and have revisited their past conversations.

"I told you," Yossi said to Oded after the massacre. "They really do want to kill us."

In the face of Hamas having just proved it, Oded could no longer disagree.

When Oded looks back, he realizes there were signs that this would happen, such as antisemitic books taught to Gazan students. He saw those books. Schools there really did indoctrinate a culture of hatred of Jews.

"That's a terrible way to make peace later on," Oded says.

Over the phone, he tells me his change of heart is typical.

"Many Israelis lost their hope on Oct. 7."

What about calls around the world for the war to stop—would he support a ceasefire?

In 2024, I reconnected with Oded Turbahn, now 66. Although a longtime believer in a two-state solution, he told me he doubts after Oct. 7 that it will be possible in his lifetime. He sent me this current photo.

He tells me he would not. The war, Oded says, has to be prosecuted all the way through.

Out of retribution?

No—it's the only path to long-term peace.

"We need to make sure Hamas is out," Oded says, "and then maybe we can find someone we can negotiate with." Hamas, says Oded, are Jihadists who will forever want to kill all "infidels," especially Jews.

What about the Palestinian civilian deaths? Shouldn't there be a pause in fighting for that?

"I don't like what happened to the civilians in Gaza," he says. "I hate it. But I don't think we should stop. We need to dismantle Hamas completely, take all the terrorists out."

It's revealing hearing that from a one-time peacenik.

I brought up a claim by the Israeli right-wing—that polls say most Palestinians feel Oct. 7 was justified. Even with Hamas gone, is negotiation possible with people who supported them?

Peace, Oded says, is by definition made with enemies. It worked for Israel with Egypt and Jordan after wars. In those cases, both sides were willing to give something up—Israel surrendering conquered land and their neighbors recognizing Israel's right to exist.

Oded has faith that such peace could be made with more moderate Palestinian leadership. But he's no longer sure that's a majority view in Israel.

"I have friends who say, 'Do you really think you can do that with Palestinians who worked for you on Saturday, and the next Saturday came and killed you?'"

Has he ever seen the divide between Jews and Palestinians this wide?

"No. This is the toughest situation."

After the intifada ended in 1993, he remembers watching from his patrol Jeep as folks in Gaza shopped, socialized, and went about their lives.

"And I said to myself at that time, 'What am I doing here? It's their country. I don't want to be there. Let them grow it up.'"

That's why he was in favor when Israel left in 2005, even though it uprooted his friend Yossi and other settlers.

"I thought, the people in Gaza can now build for themselves a very nice country," he recalls.

"Were you surprised," I ask, "that Gaza instead became a...."

"...terrorist camp? Yes, I was."

Then Oded gets a bit emotional.

"For God's sake, why?" he asks. "What is the reason they took all this aid and instead of building a country, they threw missiles at us and built tunnels? Why? I don't understand."

He feels the same about Hezbollah on Israel's northern border.

"Lebanon is an unbelievably nice country," says Oded. "Tourists from Israel would spend so much money there. Instead, they're sending missiles to try to kill us for God's sake. What does that get them?"

Why, he asks, does both Hamas and Hezbollah want only war with Israel?

Then he answers: "I know what my friend Yossi would say. Because they don't want Israel to exist."

Is Yossi right?

"I still don't want to accept it. I want to accept that people want to live in peace." He adds in a quieter voice: "But maybe I'm wrong. Maybe they don't want to live in peace."

Is there a part of him, after his years of being targeted in Gaza on patrols, that hates Palestinians?

Not at all. He points out that while running the Dollar Shave Club factory in Israel until a few years ago, his deputy was an Israeli-Arab, as were 20 percent of his employees. Jews and Arab-Israelis have good relations, even now during the war.

"What I hate," says Oded, "is that Hamas doesn't understand we have to find a way to live together."

I press him a final time. Is peace in his lifetime possible? Honest answer.

"I am afraid that the answer is no." Most Palestinians, he says, refuse to recognize Israel.

"You need two for Tango," says Oded.

Would he like to someday go back to Gaza?

Not anymore.

"The seaside in Gaza is beautiful," he says. "So many lovely beaches. They could have hosted tourists and built the economy."

But Hamas preferred killing Jews.

So it's now destroyed.

As, says Oded Turbahn, is the hope for peace—for a very long time.

While walking through a Gaza refugee camp in 1991, in Rafah, a group of curious kids clustered around me. I asked if any had thrown stones. "Of course," said one boy." Didn't that put them in danger? "Yes but I want a state." (Photo by Mark Patinkin)

ELEVEN

AMONG GAZANS...BEFORE

It is perhaps this war's most challenging story to report—hearing what Gaza is like from the people inside it. International journalists aren't allowed to go in independently. The best route would be with humanitarian groups, but they're prohibited by Israel from bringing us.

The only option is remote.

So, with the help of able Jerusalem reporters such as Isabel Debre of the Associated Press, I began to gather phone numbers.

Most shared with me had the familiar 972 Israel prefix, but a few were 970. I had to look that up on WhatsApp's dropdown list.

Palestine.

It turns out it has its own country code.

Now I begin to dial numbers.

I try Shifa Hospital's Dr. Mohammed Abu Selmia. No answer, nor to a follow-up text.

Next, Dr. Suhaila Tarazi, head of al-Ahli Hospital. The same.

As I keep dialing, my mind goes to a time during that 1991 trip when I did see Gaza from the Palestinian side. Many things, of course, have changed in the decades since then, but much has not. It could even be argued that what I saw in 1991 was a glimpse into what Gaza was like until Oct. 7.

To get inside the strip on that long-ago November, without IDF supervision, I began by hiring an Arab cab driver in Jerusalem. Israelis, with their yellow license plates, would be targets. My American passport got me through IDF's checkpoint, and after driving through empty Gaza territory, we pulled into an isolated service station where I'd arranged to meet a local guide.

As my cab turned around and headed away, a slight young man in Western clothes approached from his parked car.

"I am Ismail," he said. His English was good—he went to college in America. He welcomed me to his neighborhood, and together, this time through the lens of the Palestinian side, we headed into the heart of Gaza.

It is as if we'd gone back in time. In some areas, donkey carts outnumbered cars. This being noonish, businesses were closed in protest of Israeli occupation; a daily part of the intifada. Ismail told me most preferred staying open, but the extremists who formed the 1991 version of Hamas were in charge and would crack down.

There was anti-Israeli graffiti on most walls, some of it painted over by Jewish soldiers with black X's, but it was hard to keep up. Everywhere, there was litter.

"It used to be clean," said Ismail.

Why no longer?

"The intifada."

The litter was another form of protest—if Gazans weren't allowed to run their own land, they shouldn't take care of it. Ismail saw that as more self-punishment, but the militants decreed it.

We drove by various refugee camps: Nuseirat, 30,000 people; Bureij, 30,000; Maghazi, also 30,000. They'd been there almost 45 years, so most were like the camp I would see in Bethlehem in 2024—slum cities instead of tents.

Today—all are still there.

Soon, we arrived in the Rafah camp, stopped the car and walked onto a sandy side street. Up ahead, a group of children were playing marbles in the dust. We approached them, and since I stood out as non-Palestinian, a dozen gathered around. Gaza has one of the world's highest birth rates, and kids were everywhere, and curious.

They gave us their names, and I wrote down a few: Nidal, Asman, Fathi, Mahmud. They were a mix of ages, 6 and 7, some 8 and 10, several 12 and 14.

Through Ismail, I started to ask questions.

"Do you know what the intifada is?"

"Stones," said one named Tassir.

"For what?"

"For the state. For Palestine."

Have any of them thrown stones?

"Of course," said one boy.

"We all do," said another.

At who?

"The soldiers."

Isn't that dangerous?

"Yes, but I want a state."

One boy said his brother was killed by an Israeli soldier.

I asked how.

"When he was throwing stones, the army shot him. He's a martyr." The boy was proud of that. His brother was 20.

Has anyone else lost a family member?

Jamal, 17, said his brother is in prison. Others said the same.

I asked if any of them planned to continue attacking soldiers.

A half dozen voices gave the same quick answer: "Of course."

What scared them most about the soldiers? Tear gas? Bullets? Being arrested?

None of those things, said one boy. He would be proud to be a martyr.

The kids were all born in Gaza, as were most of their parents and in many cases, grandparents. Gaza is all they've known.

I turned to a boy named Ra'eed, 14, and asked what he considered his home. His answer took me aback.

"Be'er Sheva," he said

But that's in Israel, I told him.

"My father was born there," he said. "It's my home."

But you've lived in Gaza your whole life—isn't this your home?

"Be'er Sheva," he repeated.

What was Be'er Sheva like?

Beautiful, he said. Green trees, orange groves. It's beautiful.

When did he last see it?

"I've never been there."

>>> «««

With an hour of light left in the day, Ismail and I headed toward Jabalia, the largest of the camps. On our way, we passed through Gaza City, the territory's biggest urban center. But it lacked a heartbeat—cafes were closed, as was the local theater.

"It used to be enjoyable here," said Ismail. "We used to have parties. Bands when people got married. Now, you can't have music at weddings."

Why?

"Solidarity. The intifada."

I asked how banning music at weddings can help the cause.

Couldn't they protest without shutting down day-to-day life?

Ismail nodded. Many here resented it but didn't dare oppose the militants. On the other hand, plenty agreed it was a way to tell the world Gazans are in pain. "Now" was not important. They'd chosen to stop fully living until "someday" arrived. It's a mindset that's deep in the culture, and a reason behind Oct. 7, which is why Hamas called it Operation Al-Aqsa Flood. Gaza and the West Bank are not enough; the goal is Jerusalem.

Ismail and I continued on, 10 minutes later turning into an even more crowded enclave, streets no wider than alleys.

"Jabalia," said Ismail. The angriest part of Gaza.

Dusk was falling. I spotted graffiti, including a knife through a Star of David. After a few moments, Ismail stopped the car, telling me there was someone he wanted me to meet. As we walked in the near dark, cats scampered out of garbage. Groups of young men watched us from the shadows. I asked if it was safe. Ismail smiled: there was little crime here. Persecution can make any people angry, he said, but day-to-day, the Palestinian character is civil.

He opened a gate to a small house and an older man greeted us: Mohammed Musselem. He was wearing shorts and an old T-shirt. A tent was nearby. That, Ismail told me, was where Mohammed lived with his wife, the Israeli authorities having bulldozed his home.

I asked the older man why.

"My son was accused of throwing a bomb at the army."

The tent was on the grounds of his son-in-law's house—no matter the hardship, Palestinians take care of their own. It's how they get through.

Musselem was a refugee, born in Israel, fleeing in the war of 1948. It occurs to me as I write this in 2024 that few Palestinians are left who grew up in what's now Israel before its founding. But the yearning to return remains strong.

Musselem had a question for me about America's first war against Iraq's Saddam Hussein shortly before this 1991 Gaza visit:

"Why does Bush liberate Kuwait after six months and not Palestine after 42 years?" He added that he hoped the question did not offend me. He meant it with respect.

I assured him it's fine—tell me more.

"Forty-two years we are living like this," he said, "and Americans have done nothing for us."

I sat with Mohammed Musselem, who fled to Gaza during the war of 1948 and here in 1991, was living in a tent, explaining the Israelis bulldozed his home after his son was accused of throwing a bomb at the IDF. (Photo by Mark Patinkin)

I asked: Have the Arabs? I expected him to defend his brethren, but he didn't.

"No. Nothing." He went through names and countries: Libya, Jordan, Syria, Egypt, Iran, Iraq—they've done nothing for Palestinians.

"All bad," he said. "As bad as Israel."

I asked how things were in Palestine before 1948—was he friends with any Jews?

"Yes. We were neighbors."

Did he think Arabs and Jews could live together?

"We did before. We can again." But first, he said, the Palestinians must have their own homeland—as well as their previous land back. He meant Israel itself and left unsaid what that would mean for the Jews there.

His 9-year-old granddaughter stood next to us. I tried to draw her into conversation, but she was shy. In a way, it was refreshing—at last, I'd found a child who wasn't political. I asked if she liked the refugee camp.

Timidly: "Yes."

Would she go elsewhere if she could?

"My own land."

Where is that?

"Where my grandfather came from," she said, referring to Musselem. Then she described it: a green place with beautiful trees.

Her name was Tahreer—Arabic for "liberation." Her sister's name was "Palestine."

The old man asked one of the women of the house to bring tea—sweet Arabic tea with rosemary. As always among Palestinians, hospitality is a core value. Another son of his, Rafiq, 23, joined us. I turned to him and asked about Arab leaders.

"They're traitors," he said. They don't care about the Palestinians.

I told Rafiq that many Jews insist Palestinians are in these camps by their own choice, that Israel had even tried building them new housing, and they'd rejected it. Was that true?

"We don't want their houses," he said.

Why not? It would be a way out of this place.

"We won't leave this camp until we get our state."

Why not do both—leave the camp and continue a push for a homeland from a better place?

"We must keep this camp to remind the world to solve our problem."

It made you realize this was a key weapon of Palestinians: suffering. In a way, it was borrowed from the history of another people, the Jews. Just as the state of Israel grew out of the Holocaust, Palestinians are hoping a new Palestine would grow out of their own pain.

Ismail touched my forearm, pointing to his watch.

"It's 8:30," he said. "We're running out of time."

Our inn was 20 minutes away, and Gaza fell under Israeli military curfew at 9. Soon, we were back in the car, navigating down dark streets, threading our way out of Jabalia. Everywhere, there were children.

»» ««

Before dawn, I went to what Gazans called "The slave market," a chaotic scene where thousands of locals boarded buses and other pickup vehicles for long commutes to day-work in Israel.

I spent the night in Marna House and was awakened at 4 a.m. by prayers broadcast from a nearby mosque. It was just as well; in

15 minutes, Ismail was due to drive me to the Slave Market. It's the name Gazans used for a rural intersection where tens of thousands gathered each dawn to board buses into Israel for jobs through the Erez Crossing. It was part of the dependence that bound the two sides together.

At least until Oct. 7.

We began to drive in the dark, and although it was an urban neighborhood, you heard the crow of roosters. After a few miles, we started to pass young men walking along the roadside.

We stopped to pick one up.

He gave his age as 23, explaining he was bound for the Slave Market to board a bus to Tel Aviv—an hour-and-a-half ride. He had to be on the job at 6:30, so rose at 4. He did construction work, rehabbing a home. I asked: for a Jewish family?

"Yehude?" he said. "Yes." He'd been at it only a week and was grateful for the opportunity, having been out of work for six months when Israel restricted permits after the 1990 Gulf War over Saddam's invasion of Kuwait.

Our new passenger blamed both sides for Gaza's hardships, the Israelis for the restrictions, but also Palestinian leadership for embracing Saddam, a lost cause.

Did he support the PLO, the Palestinian government in exile at the time?

Oh yes, he said, but look—they drive around Tunis in their Mercedes, and when they make mistakes, we in the territories pay.

He used his wages to support his father and five brothers. I asked why his brothers needed that. He said they couldn't get permission to work in Israel because one was jailed and the others barred for being behind in taxes. And there were few jobs in Gaza.

Suddenly, we turned a corner and were there, the Slave Market. It was a tumultuous scene—a rural intersection by the Erez checkpoint in and out of Israel. It wasn't that different up until Oct. 7.

Ismail and I were surrounded by vast dirty lots with buses

rolling through dust and fog as thousands milled about. Beat-up vans were waiting for passengers—jitneys whose drivers had border passes to go into Israel. We approached one of the vans. Ten passengers were crammed inside, some smoking, some eating. They were farm workers, and didn't resent their Jewish employer, but disliked this life.

An army Jeep sped by, siren going, its windows covered with steel wire. The men here glared at it. Even Ismail, my U.S.-educated guide, tensed up at the sight of them. I asked why he would be afraid. If there was an incident, he said—like someone throwing a Molotov—he could get arrested in a sweep.

We approached a nearby car, this one with four men. They were on their way to work construction in Jaffa, a 90-minute ride. As we chatted, it came out they were second and third generation refugees from that same city. Did it bother them to be building Jewish homes on land their grandparents still claim? They shrugged—they had to live. But for some of them, the bitterness was deep.

"They treat us like slaves," one man said.

The comment touched on another theme that echoed from then until today. Among Palestinians, from everyday souls to Hamas itself, pride is a huge factor, and the Israelis often test it.

The first light of dawn came up, and it was now peak hour, the air filling with horns and fumes and the sounds of crowds. I stepped onto a bus to talk to riders and noticed an image that was out of character—a gray-haired man in western dress. He, too, was off to do construction work, explaining he used to be a teacher but when a brother was arrested for terrorism, it put restrictions on the whole family.

Was he resentful for the collective punishment?

Sad, he said. He would like to teach.

I stepped outside, and nearby, on another bus, a man stuck his head through a window, eyeing my notebook and camera.

"No one is happy," he said. "No one is happy."

Ismail kept me moving, explaining that the crowd made him nervous. But despite the resentful words, everyone seemed civil. "Salaam,"—peace—they said when I approached, and the same when I moved on.

Then something happened.

As I paused to write notes, people realized I was a western reporter and gathered to express their frustrations. Soon there were 10 of them. One man, Moussa, 36, said he was building housing for Russian immigrants—he needed the money—but was torn about it. He was helping new immigrants sink roots in land Palestinians claimed, including Jewish settlements in the West Bank. But his family had to eat. That, he said, was the kind of choice you must face if you are Palestinian.

I pointed out that the Russian Jews felt driven from their native land, too. Didn't that make him sympathize?

No comparison, said Moussa.

Now 30 people were gathered, then 50, and some began to get angry. No comparison, others nearby said. Here I am, one told me, building houses on land his grandfather fled in '48.

The anger got louder, and now there was shouting.

"You American journalists have done nothing for us," an older man said.

Ismail pulled at my sleeve. "Let's get out of here."

"What have you done for us?" said the man. "Nothing. Nothing."

Ismail was now physically backing me away. "There's so many crazy people," he said. "It happens—crowds, emotion, they can explode."

We headed back to our car. Buses roared by. The morning sky was smoke and rose. The ground was littered with plastic coffee cups, and the air with frustration.

I would later realize this was the key crossing that Hamas went through in the Oct. 7 attack that led to the war I would return to write about in 2024.

»» ««

The two of us drove to another refugee camp called Al-Shati—also known as The Beach Camp. It was established in 1948 for 23,000 Palestinians who fled from places like Jaffa and Be'er Sheva in Israel, squeezed into a space of a half square mile. By 2023, it would have over 90,000.

Since Gaza is only 25 miles long, it wasn't hard to visit points throughout it in a day, from Rafah in the south to the Gaza City area in the north, where I walked through the Jabalia and Al Shati refugee camps and stayed in the Marna House inn.

Part of it bordered the Mediterranean, and Ismail and I made our way to the shore. The beach was lovely, a prime spot for development. But the waterfront was lined with shabby buildings. Although the days I spent in Gaza were hot, I saw almost no one on the beaches. Ismail explained that would be considered a display of joy, and joy was frowned upon while martyrs were dying during the intifada. He seemed to roll his eyes at the self-punishment.

We paused at the camp's open-air market—tables filled with grapes, chickpeas, lentils, eggplant, and peppers. Shoppers bustled. It was an uplifting moment of normalcy and seeming safety. Except Ismail told me that in Gaza anything can happen.

"There was a confrontation here last week," he said. He meant among Palestinians of differing views. "Three people got killed."

»» ««

We stopped back at Marna House, sitting at its shaded veranda for lunch. It said much that in 1991, in a land of 700,000, this was the only hotel catering to outsiders. That would change over the decades as Gaza grew to two million, with other hotels built, some on the water. Parts of Gaza would even become upscale. Sadly, most of that development has been destroyed in the current war.

This day, I was the only guest at Marna House.

We were served by Mounzir, the chef's 14-year-old son, a sweet boy who seemed thrilled to wait on us. I mentioned to Alya Shawa, the middle-aged proprietress, how accommodating he was.

"It is the Palestinian culture," she told me. "Even if a family is poor, they will give all they have to a guest. We are happy if they are happy."

Marna House had long been a destination for notables and journalists. A few months before me, an accomplished Washington Post correspondent named Nora Boustany stayed here and wrote of how Aliya, the same proprietress, showed her an old album of Gaza social events decades before.

"Lithe Gazan women wearing strapless and low-cut evening gowns from more prosperous and tranquil times," Nora's article said. "These same women now hastily cover their heads when pulling up to a traffic light so as not to be pelted with tomatoes in disapproval."

Nora Boustany grew up in Beirut and was a pioneering female foreign correspondent, including in combat zones. She worked for *The Post* for 30 years. She had another telling observation about Gaza in that 1991 article.

"The people," she wrote, "are crammed into eight vast refugee camps and neighboring villages, often five or six to a room with nothing but thin, narrow mattresses on the floor serving as beds at night and sofas by day. The decades of Israeli occupation, neglect by Arab states, and relentless population growth have converted Gaza into one of the Middle East's most explosive trouble spots—a political and socioeconomic disaster area that is likely to be a source of instability for years to come."

That same paragraph could have been written about Gaza a decade later, two decades, and even just before Oct. 7.

After lunch, I leafed through the Marna House guest book. Aside from journalists, many who signed it were government representatives.

"All the delegates come here," Alya said. "They promise to give aid. They think if they spread a little money, the problems would be done. But we do not need that. The people can survive on bread. What they want is their freedom."

Aren't the Arab delegates committed to your cause?

"They're all rubbish," said Aliya.

But I thought Arab countries were Gaza's friends?

"No," she said. "Palestinians have no friends."

>» «<

Before I left Gaza, I wanted to capture its nonpolitical side, so I stopped by the local office of Save the Children, a U.S. humanitarian group. An American woman named Heather Grady, age 32, who headed the office, escorted me into the field. She told me the poverty here was not as bad as some of the world's more deprived nations she had worked in. Look on top of the homes here, she said: most have TV antennas. But Gazans, she added, were still destitute. Beneath those antennas, in these small 3-room houses, there were often 10 people.

I asked what Palestinians are like. Heather had never known a people that dotes on children so much. But they grow up quickly here, she added.

"Palestinian 4-year-olds know more about politics than American 30-year-olds," she said. "Children here talk about James Baker." He was secretary of state under the first George Bush. "How many American children know who James Baker is?"

I told Heather that from the news, it could seem the children of Gaza existed only to throw stones and frankly, I had experienced some of that. Could she show me those filling their days in more hopeful ways?

Yes—and we drove to something called the Bureij Sports Program. It was in the courtyard of a school building in the heart of a refugee camp. A few dozen children played soccer in colorful T-shirts. I sat with the sports director, who gave his name as Usama, age 28.

What, I asked, was the goal of the program?

"So the kids will not waste their lives."

What would they do without this?

"They would be in the streets," said Usama.

Doing what?

"Throwing stones." But this place gave them a chance at normalcy.

I spoke to another counselor, Abdul Moti, 31, a career teacher. He was here, he said, because he wanted these kids to have a childhood—ride bikes, eat ice cream, play soccer. He tried to teach them that all children are the same—Palestinians, Americans, Israelis. He'd rather have them learn that than hatred.

It seemed I had at last found an example in Gaza of how kids can leave politics behind. I asked to speak with some of the children and was soon sitting with a half dozen, ages 10 to 13. They seemed thrilled at the attention and nervous. There was none of the proud defiance of the kids I'd met on the street.

What did they like most about the program?

"Soccer," said Eyad.

"Just playing," said Hassan.

Why, I asked, do you come here?

"The streets are trouble," said Ali.

And what do you want to be?

A doctor, said one. A teacher, said another. A counselor, said a third.

So none of you throw stones?

"I have," one said.

And another said the same, and another and another.

"Isn't that dangerous?"

"We are defending our homeland."

Another asked if he could sing a song. I was relieved—a camp song I presumed.

He stood. "The day is coming," he sang, "no doubt it's coming. The morning's coming. The morning of our freedom."

What, I asked a boy named Ali, do you daydream about?

"Having my own homeland."

I turned to Ayad. "What times do you feel happy?"

"When we get back our land."

I asked Moyed his favorite way of having fun

"Thinking about our homeland."

I walked outside with another counselor who seemed to under-stand what I was trying to do.

"We want them to be carefree, too," he said. "In America, that's possible. It's not possible here. They are in refugee camps, and there are Israeli soldiers, and their uncles are getting arrested, and it's not possible."

Before I left, I paused in the courtyard to watch the children a final time. I still remember that image; young Palestinian boys, so full of joy for that one brief moment in their matching, colorful shirts.

This is the world today of Salwa Tibi and countless other Gazans displaced by war, living in tents that stretch for miles, many cobbled together with tarps and sacks. Salwa took this photo for me shortly after we messaged in early June, 2024.

TWELVE

THEN ... AND NOW

It was not hard to track down Heather Grady in 2024—she's now vice-president of Rockefeller Philanthropy Advisors. But it took a while to reach her since she was in China when I first tried. Finally, I caught her at her home in San Francisco before she headed back to Asia. Now in her 60s, she came across as I remembered her—gracious, thoughtful, and engaged in the world's challenges.

Heather went to Smith College and in 1989, after working for Save the Children in Sudan, moved to Gaza at age 30 for an almost four-year assignment, which is when we met. Her next job was with Oxfam in Vietnam, and she surprised me with an interesting memory. For her first holiday from her new post, she and her husband decided to go back to Gaza.

I told her it seemed an unlikely place to vacation.

In fact, she said, her years there were meaningful and fulfilling. Plus, the intifada had just ended, and Heather wanted to see the strip during a time of normalcy.

"There weren't curfews," she recalled of that 1994 visit, "there weren't strikes. It felt wonderful and open." She added: "What was sad is it didn't last that long."

The second intifada began in 2000 and went five years, a reminder that Gaza has often been in upheaval. Before Oct. 7, there were two smaller wars in 2008 and 2014, and Israeli incursions in 2012 and 2021, with thousands killed.

Yet Heather remembers Gaza fondly.

"It's true there's been a lot of misery and poverty," she told me, "but historically, it was a beautiful place."

Indeed, Gaza City is one of the world's oldest urban centers, first settled 5,000 years ago. In the Bible, it's where Samson pulled down the temple of the Philistines.

But what drew Heather back for that holiday were Gazans themselves.

"I always found the people there gracious and warm," she said.

When I asked what she did for fun during her years in Gaza, it got a chuckle.

"I remember exercising to Jane Fonda videos in our house."

Because of Israeli occupation, curfews, and the intifada, public recreation was seen as unseemly. Heather would take walks by the sea, but not too far because it was uncomfortable going past Israeli guard posts where guns were pointed at passersby.

Did she at least go to the beach by the Mediterranean?

Only to buy from fishermen.

Nor were there many restaurants at the time. But there were lots of shared meals with Palestinian friends, who loved to talk politics.

She and her husband had a new daughter, only five weeks old when they arrived in 1987. It wasn't hard to find a loving nanny in so child-oriented a culture. Heather recalls an exceptional collective spirit among Gazans—a contrast with America, which she finds more individualistic.

I told Heather I was struck by how there are no homeless in Palestinian culture.

"It's the same with elderly people," she said. "You don't put them off somewhere. Duty to others is very strong. I think that's what's gotten them through many decades of difficult times—reliance on each other."

I asked Heather how, when she was there, she would have predicted Gaza's future.

"Not what's happening now," she said.

Back then, she felt there would have been a Palestinian state long before 2024.

"Maybe neither side would be completely satisfied," she said, "but there would be a compromise, and a solution."

She no longer has as much hope for that.

"I don't think Israel wants a two-state solution," Heather told me. At least not the government.

She made a comparison with Northern Ireland, where, after 77 years of conflict between Catholics and Protestants, peace was made in 1998. Today, in 2024, that's exactly the span of time that Israelis and Palestinians have been at odds since modern Israel's founding in 1947. But Heather sees the two sides further apart than in 1991.

How does she view the current war?

"It's an enormous tragedy and it can be stopped," Heather said. "I think we need responsibility taken on both sides."

I pressed her on who she feels is most at fault.

She paused for a moment, mindful her work requires diplomacy, then said: "There are a lot more deaths on the Palestinian side."

And the destruction, she added, is heartbreaking. Before Oct.

7, she told me, photos of Gaza showed some nice boulevards and developed waterfront areas despite deprivations elsewhere. That's now destroyed.

I asked if she had kept in touch with Gazans she worked with.

She did on and off, and hoped to visit some in 2008 when she went on a mission to Israel with a half dozen women leaders. The others were allowed into Gaza for a day trip, but the Israelis barred Heather, never explaining why.

"I think it was because I lived there for three and half years," she told me. "Maybe I was seen as someone sympathetic to Palestinians—maybe too sympathetic. I was sad about that."

One of those she had planned to visit in Gaza was a former staffer named Salwa Tibi, a young Save the Children project officer in 1991.

"She was warm and smart and a go-getter," Heather said of Salwa. "Very active and conscientious. Great sense of humor."

In fact, Heather told me, I almost certainly met Salwa during my own visit.

Salwa, she said, is still there.

Since part of this book involves seeking those I crossed paths with 33 years ago, I decided to try to find her.

>>> «««

Salwa Tibi, 22 in 1991, is 55 today, a mother of five and grandmother of over a dozen. She has spent 35 years as a humanitarian worker in her native Gaza. Although the agencies she has worked for didn't share employee contact information, I managed to track down Salwa's mobile number elsewhere. Her WhatsApp profile picture is of yellow flowers. I tried calling but I didn't get through.

Yet Salwa Tibi's voice has surfaced often, and through her many online postings, I gained a glimpse into what everyday Gazan souls like her have endured over decades.

One month after the current war began, on Nov 3, 2023, I

found a post from Salwa saying the basics of life were being lost.

"Whether a safe place," she said, "clean water, food, clothes, blankets, diapers."

By then, Salwa and her family had fled their home in the north, heading 20 miles south to Rafah, where things had deteriorated.

"It's becoming dangerous to go out and get bread," she said in that Nov. 3 post. Folks she knew had been injured in an Israeli airstrike while waiting in line.

Salwa and 14 of her displaced family members found an apartment to rent in Rafah, where they were living on dwindling canned food.

"There is no bread at all, due to the lack of flour," she reported. "My message to the world is to stop the war, as we love life."

Around that same time, a freelancer for Britain's *I-News* named Jessie Williams connected with both Salwa and her 29-year-old daughter, Nedaa Abu Rsas, for an article published on that same Nov. 3.

Nedaa told *I-News* she had to walk half a mile through shelling with her 2-year-old daughter Nalya and 4-month-old son Yazan—Salwa's grandchildren—to reach temporary shelter at a hospital.

Now, in the crowded Rafah apartment, Nedaa's husband had just heard that their home in the north was badly damaged.

"I don't know where I will go," Salwa's daughter told *I-News*.

Nor was there enough water—Salwa said no one in the apartment had been able to shower in 16 days.

Salwa told *I-News* this was the fourth time she'd been displaced during that first month of war. The bombing, she said, was worse at night, so everyone was trying to sleep during the day.

"We have faced a lot of wars and aggression in Gaza," Salwa said, "but nothing like this one. This is the hardest."

I saw another communication from Salwa posted Nov. 28, during the week-long ceasefire following the exchange of 105 Israeli hostages for 240 Palestinians from Israeli jails.

"The best thing in the last few days was to finally see the children smile again," Salwa reported of the lull. "I walked with them on the street—I wanted them to see the sun, the light, the good parts of life."

During that walk, Salwa ran into friends who couldn't afford the pricey food in the open-air market.

"All they had were the clothes they were wearing when they had to leave their homes," Salwa said.

So she gave them some of her own money.

"I think this is what helps us all survive," she said in the post, "the kindness we show each other. Everyone gives what they can. But most of us are displaced and have lost everything."

By now, Salwa had learned her own home up north had been destroyed.

"I worked for more than 25 years to build this house," she said. "I can't believe all this is gone now. We have lost so much, and none of us expected this to last for such a long time."

By that, she meant six weeks. And yet as I write this, Salwa has endured seven additional months of war. And counting.

I found Salwa Tibi's name again in a Dec. 14, 2023 *CNN* story. With winter temperatures in the 40s, Salwa said she had just walked miles to search for blankets despite nearby Israeli airstrikes.

"I felt bad for the kids," Salwa told *CNN*. "They had nothing to keep them warm and we were dying from the cold at night."

I came across yet another article featuring Salwa, this one on the news site *Vox*, with familiar photos of destroyed parts of Gaza.

Except in a twist reflective of life in Gaza, this story was from an earlier conflict there, in May of 2021. That one started in Jerusalem, showing the situation's complexity. When Israel moved to evict six Palestinian families from their East Jerusalem homes, tensions rose, and on May 7, Arab protesters near the Temple Mount began throwing stones at Israeli police, who then shut down the sacred Muslim area. That prompted Hamas in Gaza to send missiles into

Israel, ultimately killing 13. Israel hit back with airstrikes, and the battle went for 11 days, killing 256 Palestinians and displacing 76,000.

Salwa Tibi was among countless Gazans caught in the middle of it. *Vox* reporter Jen Kirby described what Salwa was up against this way: "Tibi hadn't been sure if she would see the next morning, so heavy was the bombardment. This week, Tibi's daughter, pregnant for the first time, gave birth in the hospital, Tibi's granddaughter Nalya entering the world to the sound of shelling."

I came across another post quoting Salwa that I again thought was current, but it was from a short Israel-Gaza war 18 years ago—a reminder of how many there have been.

That one began Dec. 27, 2008, only a year or so after Hamas took over Gaza from the Palestinian Authority. Ongoing tensions and IDF raids prompted Hamas to fire missiles, triggering an Israeli ground invasion lasting three weeks and leaving over 1,300 Palestinians dead.

Forty-eight hours into that conflict, on Dec. 29, Save the Children posted a report from Salwa.

"The situation is terrible," she said. "The Apache helicopters are precise but the F16 fighters cause widespread damage to buildings around their targets. It goes on day and night."

Her family was trying to survive in their home.

"We have to keep all the doors and the windows open otherwise they could get blown in by the bombs," Salwa said. "That means it is very cold. We have long periods without electricity."

Because of the bombing, she lamented, her staff was unable to get food from their warehouse to needy families.

"We are living from day to day," said Salwa. "There is no escape. The air strikes began just as children were leaving school, exposing them to horrific scenes of violence. They just want to be like children in other countries."

A week later, on Jan. 14, 2009, Save the Children put out

another report from Salwa after a four-hour ceasefire that Gazans hoped would last longer, but didn't.

"We heard about the ceasefire at 12:30 today," Salwa said. "It ended at 4 and at five past 4 exactly, the shelling started again."

During the lull, Salwa went to find bread, but the lines were too long.

"Three hours, believe me, is not enough," Salwa said of the ceasefire. "There were lots of people queuing. Children, women, old men, youths. Everyone was waiting."

She added an insight into the resilience of Gaza's children.

"When I was walking outside seeing the children playing football, I was very happy," said Salwa. "But only having three hours! We thought 'Come on! So quickly!' They started bombing at 4 pm exactly."

>>> <<<

As I was finishing this chapter in May of 2024, I tried Salwa again on WhatsApp, this time by text. I told her I was an American journalist writing about the war, and that we had met briefly when I interviewed Heather Grady 33 years ago.

A minute or so later, I was surprised to hear my phone buzz in Providence. By luck, I caught her in Gaza with available internet, which she said doesn't happen often these days.

"Hi Mark," Salwa texted. "Nice to hear back from you after a long time."

Unsure if our connection would last, I started right in, asking if she could describe the conditions in Gaza.

Soon, a 90-second voice message popped up. It began with a quite literal sigh.

"The situation now I can tell you, it's very terrible for everyone," Salwa said. "There is no clean water, the streets are full of sewage and garbage. Thousands of the people are living now in the tents."

Trenches were being dug as bathrooms, and the tents, she said, go for miles, many pieced together with tarps and empty sacks, packed so densely it was hard to walk among them.

A minute later my phone buzzed with a follow-up.

Salwa Tibi, who has done humanitarian work in Gaza for decades, also sent me this photo of herself before Oct. 7, in better times.

"Another story is the flies," Salwa said. "The children can't sleep in the night from the hot and the insects. Most of the people are depending on...let me call it unhealthy and unclean water. Last night I didn't sleep at all, just two hours."

Salwa said she had recently been displaced for the sixth time. She had been sheltering in Rafah to the south, but with the approach of the Israeli army there, she evacuated northward to the city of Deir el-Balah in Gaza's center.

I asked if she was still living with 15 people, as she posted a few months before.

"No," Salwa said minutes later by voice message, "it has increased. I want to tell you that now I'm living with 50 person, 15 are children, the youngest is eight months, like this."

Who, I asked, were the 50?

Her adult daughters and their many kids, as well as other women and children in her extended family. The husbands, said Salwa, were in nearby tents so the females could have a bit of dignity.

"We are living in an apartment without rooms, doors, bathroom," Salwa said. "There is no privacy."

She texted a photo of some of her young grandchildren on thin, unclean mattresses in a cinderblock room with no other furniture.

"We divided it with some material as there is no wall inside," Salwa explained.

I asked if there is any plumbing or electricity.

"No electricity at all in Gaza Strip," Salwa answered. Except for solar, but not in her building. She was lucky her humanitarian agency had solar nearby so she could power her cell.

What did her adult kids do for a living?

One of her sons ran a café in Gaza City, while another was a dentist with his own clinic.

"But they're not working now," Salwa told me, "because the clinic and café are totally damaged, and they didn't get another job due to the harsh situation, Mark."

She added: "Now, they will have to build their life from zero."

How, I asked, are the sons supporting their families?

"When I get my salary," Salwa said, "I can get them some money to take care of their children."

She added that one of her daughters-in-law was pregnant.

"Can you imagine," Salwa texted. "She will deliver the baby in the upcoming months."

Big families, I had learned, are part of Palestinian culture—Salwa herself has five brothers and two sisters. Her husband works for the Gaza Ministry of Health.

"My father is still alive," she said. "He was displaced in 1948." She meant pushed by Israel as a refugee into Gaza during the war of independence. The Palestinians have a different name for it, The Nakba—catastrophe in Arabic.

Salwa said that throughout her dad's life, he has wanted to go back. He's now housed in Gaza with one of Salwa's brothers.

"His living condition are very bad because he uses a wheelchair," she told me.

She soon sent another voice message saying that despite being in a designated evacuation area, a car nearby had been targeted in a strike. It was on the same route Salwa sometimes takes to her work.

"There is no safe place," she told me.

By now, we had been going back and forth for 45 minutes. I knew Salwa had much to do, so I moved on to a few final questions.

Does she still love Gaza?

"Of course," Salwa said. "I was born in Gaza, completed my university in Gaza. Gaza means a lot to me."

Does she plan to stay?

Her voice-message response began with another sigh. "Due to the current situation," Salwa said, "if immigration is open, I would leave Gaza. Because we are a big family, and what is happening, we don't have enough money for the children now."

I asked if there were things she dreamt of as a child.

Like many in Gaza, Salwa Tibi has been displaced by war over a half dozen times, from the Gaza City area to Rafah to Deir el-Balah.

"I'm sure you will laugh and smile when I tell you my dream was to be as a journalist," she said. "But I'm working as a humanitarian worker supporting the people because my dream had to change."

Then she apologized, saying she knew she hadn't gotten to all my questions.

"I forget some of what you asked," Salwa said, "because I am so tired."

I could hear it in her voice.

In a sign she needed to move on, she brought the conversation full circle, asking if I was in touch with Heather Grady.

Yes, I was.

Would I please say hello for her?

I promised to do so, then thanked Salwa Tibi for being so generous with her time, and in her work, and wished her peace.

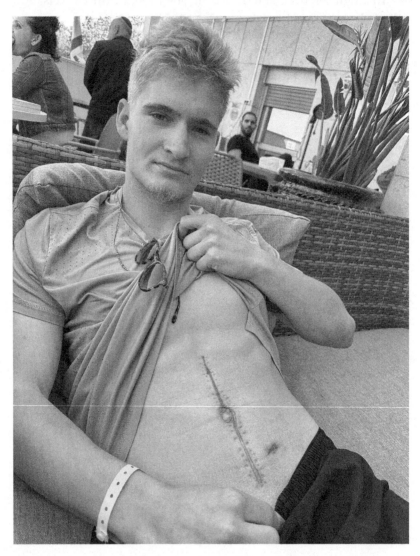

In Sheba Hospital outside Tel Aviv, Menachem Vile, 20, showed me one of his many wounds from an RPG that hit a fellow soldier and friend standing a few feet from him while the two fought in Gaza. Menachem now wears an image of his lost buddy on a dog tag around his neck. (Photo by Mark Patinkin)

THIRTEEN

THE WAR WOUNDED

It is the gathering place for Israel's wounded soldiers, a hospital patio where they come outside in wheelchairs and on crutches, and when the weather's good, there are so many it's hard to count.

If you're going to cover the war, whether here or Gaza, this is where part of the story is, in hospitals.

And so I drive toward Tel Aviv to nearby Sheba Medical Center, the biggest in the Middle East, with almost 2,000 beds. It has set aside an entire section for Gaza IDF casualties, and almost every day, helicopters bring more.

As I walk down the busy corridor to the patio, with patients in and out of their rooms, something is off that I can't put a finger on. Then I realize it. It's not natural to see so many young men in their prime in a hospital.

Menachem Mendel Vile is among them. He's 6 feet tall, blondish and 20. He has the build and manner of an athlete, but because of the shrapnel, his left hand isn't working right now. When he picks up a cardboard cup, he has to wedge it, like people who are paralyzed.

His left knee was damaged so badly you're surprised he kept the leg, but the doctors here are very good and it's doing better, despite two pieces of metal still in there.

Menachem shows me another wound, a foot-long scar where they opened him from below the navel to the chest to take out more shrapnel, as well as eight inches of small intestine. But he tells me others gave up far more, like a soldier named Uriah Yaakov whose image Menachem wears on a dog tag around his neck.

I ask who that is.

"A friend who was with me when we got hit."

"Is he OK?"

He pauses.

"He's not with us anymore." Yaacov was only 19.

Menachem's job as a soldier in Gaza was to look for booby traps and other dangers, often in houses.

"You see televisions, everything normal," he tells me. "Then you find suicide vests under a blanket."

He adds that tunnels and weapons were everywhere—hospitals, playgrounds, universities.

"It shocks you," he says. "You realize how many people are involved."

Five weeks before I met him, he was a lead soldier walking through an intersection in the Jabalia refugee camp with Yaacov next to him when there was an explosion. All Menachem remembers is being on the ground with his ears ringing and blood all over his body. Part of Menachem's intestines were out and had to be pushed back in by a medic. As he lay there, he thought to himself that this was the end.

A corridor in a large, special section of Tel Aviv's vast, 2,000 bed Sheba Hospital that had to be cleared and set aside for Israeli soldiers wounded in Gaza. (Photo by Mark Patinkin)

It turned out Hamas had fired a rocket-propelled grenade, and his friend Yaacov took most of it, which saved Menachem's life. He would later realize pieces of Yaacov's body were on him as he lay there. He knows he is sharing a graphic image, but he tells me it's what war is like.

Around us, others move in and out of the patio, many in wheelchairs. They all seem to know each other, and it's clear this space is an important part of their recovery.

Then I recognize a face I had seen in the news. It's Mia Schem, age 21, among the hostages released Nov. 30, 2023, after 55 days in Hamas captivity. She is still recovering at Sheba. She had been shot in the arm and then kidnapped from the Nova festival. The bullet damaged a bone, and she had not been treated properly in captivity, so is here for another operation.

At the moment, she's at a table talking with fellow patients—all of them soldiers. Her mother Keren Schem is with her. Soon after the prisoner exchange, both had spoken to the media about Mia being held by a captor and his wife in a private home. They gave her no painkillers for her wound, and she had to change dressings herself. On some days, she wasn't given any food. Before her release, she was in a deep tunnel where it was hard to breathe.

I approach Keren. Would she and Mia by chance want to talk?

Keren is gracious, giving me a smile. But she says her daughter had been exhausted by those earlier interviews, and isn't quite ready for that again. I can see Keren isn't either. There is a deep weariness in her eyes. In the following month, the two would be more public, even coming to America in March to speak about what Mia had gone through, and the importance of remembering the hostages. But at this point, she needed to just be in the sun with others on the patio of the wounded and focus on healing.

I sit back down with Menachem and ask what he's taken from what happened to him.

"Nothing's a given," he says. "A friend you just laughed with—10 minutes later they might not be here."

And he appreciates everything now, even saying his non-working left hand is a blessing, because at least he still has it.

Then he tells me what helps him most. Sometimes, he looks toward Tel Aviv, where people are working, biking and out enjoying restaurants. Instead of resenting it during this time of sacrifice, he is glad life goes on. That, he says, is why soldiers do what they do, so their country can have normalcy.

»» ««

With three-plus months now passed since Oct. 7, I doubted any of the wounded from that terrible day would still be at Sheba.

But there is one left.

Her name is Ellay Golan, 34, and the two of us are now sitting in the hospital's atrium. There's an indent below Ellay's neck where they had to intubate because of what the burns did to her lungs. She wears two pressure gloves for healing, and the almond skin on her arms is now discolored.

The burns cover more than half her body, and the issues from smoke inhalation were worse. It happened after Hamas set fire to her home in Kibbutz Kfar Azza, which was among the worst hit. Sixty people were murdered there, and 18 kidnapped into Gaza.

Having been in Israel for over a week, I am by now familiar with the name Kfar Azza. Along with "Be'eri" and "Nir Oz," it was among Israel's Pearl Harbors, the villages where the war started.

Ellay is a new doctor thinking of internal medicine or gynecology. Her husband, Ariel, is a social worker, who, during the same attack, was burned over 40% of his body. Their daughter, Yael, is 1½, and the number for her is 30% because her parents shielded her from the flames with their own selves.

The way bomb shelters often work in Israeli homes is you pick an existing room and reinforce it to code. Rockets from Gaza were so frequent at Kfar Azza that Ellay and Ariel chose their daughter's bedroom so they wouldn't have to wake her every time.

Around 6:30 a.m. on Oct. 7, because of missiles, they retreated there again. Except this time, the missiles didn't stop, and soon they heard automatic weapons fire. Kfar Azza is only a mile from the Gaza border. They were shocked to see through a window that men were outside, trying to get into the house. Ellay noticed they had no guns. She would later realize they were civilians who decided to run through the holes in the Gaza fence and join the slaughter.

I arrived at Israel's biggest hospital 100-plus days after Oct. 7, and was surprised that a few of the wounded were still patients, including Ellay Golan, recovering from burns after invaders trapped her family in their home and set fire to it. (Photo by Mark Patinkin)

It took hours for them to break into the house, but they persisted and finally did. At that point, Ellay's husband Ariel sent what he thought would be his final message to the family's chat group.

"Pray for us," it said. "They're inside. Goodbye."

Realizing where the family was hiding, the invaders tried to force their way into the secure room. Somehow, Ariel was able to hold the door handle firmly enough to stop them.

The attackers then set a fire in the house. Smoke began to suffocate Ellay, Ariel and Yael. They had no choice but to move through another door into their adjoining bedroom, which was further from the smoke. Ariel worked to barricade that room, too.

From where they were outside, the attackers saw where the family now was. They got hold of a propane tank, opened the gas, and lit the venting fumes. Then they threw the tank through the bedroom window. It set off flames everywhere, scorching all three of the Golans. That was the goal, to burn them alive. The parents huddled around Yael to take most of the flames with their own bodies. They also tried to stay low to the ground, where the smoke wasn't as severe.

At that point, they retreated into the bathroom, with Ariel again holding the door shut while Ellay kept fabric on her daughter's mouth but not her own. One of the men outside drove a pole through the bathroom's glass window that struck Ellay in the forehead. It was complete chaos.

Here in Sheba Hospital, I ask Ellay how she persevered while inhaling smoke and with so much of her skin burned.

"I don't know how to explain it," she tells me. "Just adrenaline. We fought to save our daughter."

Suddenly, one of the men said in Arabic that soldiers might be coming, and miraculously, they left.

But it took hours more to be rescued. The three of them went outside and hid in the closed cab of a big kibbutz tractor, crouching beneath the windows. They hoped it was the kind of place the militants would not suspect.

Finally, Israeli soldiers took the Kibbutz back from the terrorists and the three were flown by helicopter to Sheba Hospital's burn unit. Ellay's brother Evyatar Hogeg was soon there.

"Seeing her was a relief," he later said, "but seeing her burned alive was hard."

He would later say on a hospital video that being touched personally by such atrocities convinced him that the people who did this were more interested in blood than freedom.

After 48 hours in Sheba, Hamas missiles began targeting the area, so Ellay and other critical patients were moved to a reinforced underground ward where their care would not be interrupted by such attacks.

Ellay was not expected to survive. She needed to be placed in a medical coma for two months—that's how bad the lung damage was. She also needed extensive debridement of the dead skin around her burns. At one point, Ellay's lungs and heart began to fail, and she was put on an ECMO machine, a form of life support. She had to stay on it for many weeks.

Her husband Ariel was also placed in an induced coma. There is a video of him waking up in his hospital room thinking he was still under attack.

The first word he says is, "Shooting?"

"There's no more shooting," a nurse tells him. "It's over, Ariel."

Days later, when he was more able, Ariel was brought to see his daughter, who was being treated nearby. That moment was captured on video, as well. It's joyful to watch him reach for her, but also difficult since little Yael had burn bandages on her arms, hands and head.

Over many weeks, Ariel, still a patient himself, would walk with crutches to sit by his wife Ellay, who remained unconscious. He would whisper to her, "Please come back to us."

To the surprise of some of the medical staff, Ellay persevered, and did.

Before saying goodbye, I ask Ellay what she thinks will happen between Israel and the Palestinians.

She tells me they lived on the kibbutz because they believed in coexistence.

Now?

She says she can't forget that those who tried to kill her family weren't Hamas, but Gaza civilians.

Then she says, "I don't know if we have people anymore to do peace with."

»» ««

As I sit on the soldiers' patio, I continue to be struck by how young they look. Later this day, I would interview an army doctor named Scott Ehrenberg, 34, who had the same reaction, though in his case, it was while treating fellow troops in Gaza.

Scott grew up in Great Neck, New York, and moved to Israel at 18, in part because his grandparents were death camp survivors, and through them, he saw the need for Jews to have a safe place.

Soon after the ground war began, Scott was assigned to treat the wounded just outside Gaza as a combat doctor with a tank and infantry division. His wife, Elisheva, was weeks from having their first child, but he had to say goodbye to her.

During his first days, Scott's work as a war doctor was almost nonstop as Israel sent waves of troops to unsecured areas in the strip. Hamas militants were well dug in, coming out of tunnels, firing RPGs and anti-tank missiles.

The wounded began to arrive in bunches, often four at a time, then two more along with another two who weren't breathing. They wouldn't be considered dead until a doctor like Scott declared them.

As an internist, Scott was used to treating older folks. This couldn't have been more different, with most soldiers in their young 20s. Scott and his team would scissor off uniforms, manage airways, give fluids for low blood pressure and work to stop bleeding. As soon as they stabilized the latest for transfer to hospitals, more would arrive.

"I began to think, 'Make it stop,'" Scott tells me. "'Enough.'" But it didn't stop. It went like that throughout each shift and beyond, from 8 a.m. until 9 at night.

I ask about those who weren't breathing when they reached him. What was the protocol for declaring soldiers dead?

Dr. Scott Ehrenberg, who grew up in Great Neck, N.Y., told me of the nonstop stream of wounded and dead Israeli soldiers flowing through his field unit the first days of the war. "Make it stop," he kept thinking, "enough." His wife Elisheva gave birth to their son Itamar soon after the war started. (Photo by Mark Patinkin)

He tells me the signs are usually clear—no pulse, pupils nonreactive to light, no heartbeat, no blood pressure, and grave damage, such as deep shrapnel and gunshot wounds. Scott would do all he could, but few in such condition could be saved or revived. So he would declare them, thinking, "I'm so sorry you had to be the one." He'd watch as a special team zipped each body into a white bag, then loaded them into a truck, and soon, he knew, the families would be getting a knock on their door.

At one point between patients, Scott stepped away and wept, apologizing to his commander, who assured him there was no need, it showed he was a human being. The commander told Scott the soldiers died so the people of Israel could live.

Scott was able to come home for the arrival of his son Itamar, but had to return to Gaza soon after. On the 31st day after the birth, in keeping with Jewish custom, Scott led a ceremony inside Gaza sanctifying a firstborn son. He was surrounded by fellow soldiers.

"I am standing in front of you as a new father," he told the gathering, "and I can say that I have the privilege of being a doctor and a soldier in this battalion. On October 7th, our enemy tried to hurt us, to destroy us. But they did not succeed. The fact that we are standing here initiating another member into the next generation of Jews, to me, is a symbol of victory."

He went on: "As a Jew, as an Israeli citizen, and as a grandson of four Holocaust survivors that all endured the concentration camps, I believe we will win this war and will continue to thrive. I am dedicating this ceremony to those that were killed in Be'eri, Nir Oz, Kfar Azza, the Nova Festival, and all the heroes who have fallen since the beginning of the war."

Not long after the ceremony, Scott was back to work treating the wounded and declaring the dead.

»» ««

On the patio of the wounded, David, an Orthodox Jew, and Razi, an Arab-Israeli soldier, saw each other and embraced. They'd bonded over each losing a finger in the war. David calls Razi, "My holy brother." (Photo by Mark Patinkin)

I did one final interview before I left the Sheba Hospital patio, this time with an Israeli Druze soldier. His name is Sgt. Major Razi, 26, and he plans to be career military with the IDF. On Nov. 13, an RPG exploded next to him, and months later, he's still in Sheba on a crutch. He also lost a finger.

Druze are Arabs, so I ask why he wants to serve in the Army.

Israel is his home, says Razi. "I want to serve and defend my country."

But is Israel oppressing Palestinians—his fellow Arabs?

No, says Razi, they started this war. "If they change, and want peace, we'll have peace."

And then there comes a lovely moment.

An Orthodox Jewish soldier named David spots Razi. David has also lost part of a finger in the war and, like Razi, is due for more surgery.

He is thrilled to see Razi. Here on the patio of the wounded, they'd forged a friendship over their similar loss.

"My holy brother," says David.

And then the two embrace.

One of the larger-than-life Israelis I met was Mike Ginsberg, who moved from Flatbush, N.Y. to a kibbutz on the border with Lebanon, which he pointed out to me in here in 1991. (Photo by Mark Patinkin)

FOURTEEN

THE OTHER BORDER

A nd then there is the other border.

The one to the north by Lebanon, where Hezbollah has been sending missiles into Israel, displacing 80,000 souls.

I assumed Mike Ginsberg was among them. He is one of the most memorable Israelis I've known—brash, born in America, and though not overly religious, felt he was meant to be in the land of the Bible.

He lived in Kibbutz Misgav Am, where, if you poked your arm through its security fence, your hand would basically be in Lebanon.

I met him on that 1991 trip and even then, Hezbollah missiles occasionally came his way. That's the kind of neighborhood Israel has long been in, but no one, Mike Ginsberg felt, has the right to tell Jews where they can live in their own land. So there he was, in the Upper Galilee.

A hundred pioneering families established Misgav Am in 1945, three years before modern Israel was born. They raised avocados and kiwis, farmed fish and in time built a factory that still today makes bandages and wound dressings. Like the kibbutzim near Gaza, Misgav Am is surrounded by a security fence, its entry gate the kind you find outside prisons. Mike Ginsberg was my reception committee. He is a big man, 40ish at the time, who told me he emigrated 20 years before from America.

I asked why he'd want to move from the safety of the states to here.

I am a Jew, he said; this is where I belong.

On his belt were a walkie talkie and a handgun. Part of his job, he explained, was guard duty. He took me to an overlook.

"That's Lebanon," he said, pointing through the barbed wire. "Those villages are Shiite. Pay attention, we're going to have a quiz later on." He paused to light a cigarette, but the wind up here at 2700 feet made it impossible, and he gave up.

He pointed to our right, beyond Mt. Hermon, at 9,000 feet the tallest point in Israel.

"That's Syria," said Mike. "We're right between Lebanon and Syria."

Both are hostile neighbors, and there is at times a dark humor around that here. Often, Mike said, Jewish soldiers at observation posts will wave to the enemy through binoculars.

As we walked toward the center of the kibbutz, I asked Mike where he was born.

"Flatbush," he said. In Brooklyn. Today, it's gentrified, but it wasn't when Mike grew up. "It's where I got my basic training."

I asked about his sidearm.

"It's a CZ," he said—Czech made. "I took it from one of them."

Them?

"A PLO officer." Palestinian Liberation Organization. Ginsberg served as a soldier during the war of Lebanon of 1982. There was another such war in 2006.

Why did he carry the gun now, when he wasn't on guard duty? It's not as if he was full-time military.

"The difference between us and Israeli officers," he told me, "is they get 48 hours when they're called for duty. We get two seconds."

As we sat on the kibbutz green, Mike said the border used to be a friendly one—Jews and Arabs going back and forth at times.

"It was a cup of sugar relationship." That ended around 1970 when Palestinians flooded Lebanon after the Jordanian army slaughtered and expelled many thousands.

"You don't read about that much," Mike said. "God forbid for a Jew to raise his hand against one Arab, but when an Arab kills 25,000 Palestinians, it's nobody's business."

Ginsberg does not buy his clothes from Armani; he wore an old blue t-shirt and pants with the seam split at the knee. Behind him, two kids went by on bikes. A dog walked up and sat down. Two men strolled past carrying rifles.

By 1975, Ginsberg recalled, Israel's knee-high border fence with Lebanon was no longer good enough. Palestinian terrorists, he said, had decided the Jews here should be driven out. So 80 miles of high barbed wire went up.

"It's not nice living inside a barbed wire fence," he told me, "especially for Jews. Even though it was meant to keep the other guys out instead of us in."

But the fence couldn't keep out rockets. Hezbollah's favorite back then was a hand-held variety called a Katyusha.

"You ever sit in a bomb shelter with little kids all night?" Mike asked. "You don't want to."

He told a story to explain why it was hard to stop the rockets.

He was on Army patrol in Lebanon once when he came across an elderly Arab. They found four Katyushas in his carrying pack. The old man admitted he was going to fire them at Misgav Am.

"I said to him, 'Are you crazy,' " Ginsberg recalled. " 'That's where my children live.' He says to me, 'I get $250 for launching these.'"

That, Mike said, is what they are up against. How do you fight an enemy that hides behind old men? Worse, he said, Hezbollah was becoming a state within a state, beyond the control of the Lebanese government.

Then Mike began to talk about April 7, 1980.

During the early morning of that day, five terrorists cut the Kibbutz fence. They walked onto this green where we were now sitting.

"Then," Mike said, "they went into that house right there."

It was a childcare house, he explained, where babies slept under adult care, a kibbutz custom. The terrorists, he said, knew exactly where to go.

"I don't want to give the impression they were stupid. On a performance level, I have admiration for them. They knew what they were doing."

They woke the adults up. "It wasn't a good morning kiss," Mike said. "They beat them up and hog-tied them."

As dawn broke, the secretary of the kibbutz was the first to come to the house. As he opened the door, they murdered him.

The alarm went out and an Israeli army strike team came in. Inside the house, babies as young as two months old had been gathered by the militants in a single room. The Palestinians put out demands—chiefly the release of prisoners in Israeli jails.

After a long standoff, said Mike, a miracle happened. The army stormed the building and within seconds, killed every terrorist. Then a greater miracle: Parents rushed in to retrieve their babies and found them alive. Some were wounded by glass, but they were alive.

"But then," Ginsberg recalled, "one father said, 'I can't find my son.' His son was 2. And I have to tell it to you the way it is. It's hard, but I have to tell it. The child was crying, and the terrorists kept telling him to shut up. And he didn't; he was 2. So one of them walked over and smashed his head in with the butt of a rifle. They smashed in the head of a 2-year-old baby. That's what we're facing here."

He said there's a greater point.

"They talk peace. But what they say and what they do are very different things. Up here, we know what they do."

Kibbutz Misgav Am sits on the border with Lebanon, and not far from Syria, two hostile neighbors.

I asked why he didn't move his family to, say, Tel Aviv.

"This is my home. I'm not going to run."

Now I asked about peace. Would he trust a negotiated settlement? Give the Palestinians a state in return for a promise of peace?

"Let me put it this way," said Mike. "They've convinced the rest of the world, but they haven't convinced us. Almost every day, they're still trying to get through that fence. Six million Jews were killed because we were weak, and I'm not going to let it happen again. I'm not going to be brought like sheep to slaughter."

Seeing Mike Ginsberg standing here, surrounded by enemies, got me thinking back to Masada. It is important to see Masada to understand the Jews of Israel. It is a stunning fortress atop a mountainous rock tower where 900 Jewish zealots retreated up steep paths after Jerusalem was crushed by the Romans around 70 AD. It is the last place Israel's Jews would be sovereign here for 2,000 years. They established a community there on its expansive plateau of many acres, and despite being surrounded, held out for 36 months—1,400 feet above the enemy. But slowly, in an astonishing act of engineering, the Romans, over years, built a wide earthen ramp all the way to the top so they could attack. When they at last broke in, the 900 Jews who'd been defending the fortress only the day before were found dead. Convinced they'd be slaughtered or enslaved on surrender, they killed themselves first. Some historians feel they actually died in battle. Either way, it is seen here as a legendary last stand. The guide I was with there told me how Masada's spirit is evoked still. The army's elite units are initiated by hiking this summit at night, with torches and rifles, to vow that Israel shall never fall again.

And now, in an echo of that, here was Mike Ginsberg, one of 300 Kibbutz Jews surrounded by enemies, speaking of that same lesson—that if you're not strong, you'll be slaughtered. Perhaps, if I lived here on this border, I would think as he did.

But I also found myself wondering: what was the biggest risk for Mike Ginsberg? To trust that a regional peace could come from a two-state solution, or not to trust?

Then he told me of the nearby community of Ma'alot, where, in a smaller version of Oct. 7, 25 young teen students were slaughtered in May of 1974 by infiltrators.

Mike didn't doubt a Palestinian state might look peaceful at first. But what if it fell under hardliners who wanted all of Israel? He wasn't willing to take the gamble.

Of course, I met many Israelis who felt differently than Mike.

"Both of us have a case," an Israeli named Dov told me. "Both Jews and Palestinians can make a good claim. So the only hope is for both of us to swallow some pride, and trust the enemy, which isn't done easily in the Middle East. But what's our choice?"

Then Dov repeated some wisdom I'd heard from visionaries on both sides: the whole dream isn't possible for either. The only path is for each to give up part of their dream.

One night in Jerusalem, I was discussing exactly that with an Israeli cab driver when an attractive woman walked by as we sat at a stoplight. The driver, around 45, told me she symbolized the politics of the Middle East.

"Me," he said, "I no look. My wife, she is enough. You want more—more money, more women, more land, you are never happy. Happy, you must say, what I have, it is enough."

»» ««

After dinner on the kibbutz, I walked back to the green and ran into an older woman, Hana Ginsberg—Mike's mother. She was 74 and recently moved here from New York, settling into a new life between the guns of Syria and the terrorists of Hezbollah. I asked if this wasn't a hard place to live.

"My blood pressure is normal," Hana said. "Though when I hear the booms, I do get a little nervous."

How did she fill her time?

"Oh," she said, "I like to knit. And watch television. Tonight is L.A. Law."

Why did she move here?

"To be near my son and grandchildren."

Is that the only reason?

There was another: "I live in the most beautiful place on earth."

»» ««

And now, in 2024, I decide to get back in touch with Mike Ginsberg. It is painful to learn he died in March of 2006 at age 51 of a heart attack. It was hard to picture—he was a swashbuckling figure you thought would live a long life.

Mike Ginsberg is still remembered in Misgav Am.

I learned that Mike came from quite a family. In 1994, his younger brother Marc was appointed by Bill Clinton to be ambassador to Morocco, the first Jewish American named head diplomat to an Arab country.

Mike had three children with his wife Chaya, to carry on his name and spirit. But now I learned something tragic, and relevant to this book, about one of them.

Mike Ginsberg's son Eli served 22 years in the Israeli military, rising to Lieutenant Colonel. He was considered a standout soldier and leader. He retired in September 2023 at age 42. Two weeks later, he was called back to duty while Oct. 7 was still unfolding.

He and his wife Malki had four young children. Malki, a fitness trainer, would later tell the *Jerusalem Post* that their phone rang that Saturday morning of the 7th, and in 15 minutes, Mike Ginsberg's son Eli was packed and heading out. She asked him not to go, but Eli told her the country was at war—again—and he had to answer the call.

On Oct. 8, Eli was in Be'eri, the very kibbutz I had visited, to help take it back. Hamas militants were still there the day after, and Eli Ginsberg joined that battle. During it, he was killed. One account I saw said he was shot as he went into a house to rescue a family. A July 2024 report stated that an astonishing 340 Hamas members had invaded Be'eri.

"My heart is shattered into a thousand tiny pieces," Eli's wife said at his funeral. "I refuse to believe that you, the love of my life, are no longer."

I reached out to Eli's uncle, Amb. Marc Ginsberg. He said the family was not ready to be interviewed about Eli's loss.

Eli was raising his family in a kibbutz called Dovrat an hour south of his father's beloved Misgav Am. Like his dad at Misgav Am, Eli was head of security at Dovrat.

When I spent that day with Mike Ginsberg on the border with Lebanon, I might have thought that 33 years later, Israelis would not have to be as vigilant to stay safe. Oct. 7 reminds that if anything, the threat is greater. Just as Eli's loss reflects the often-generational heartbreak of being an Israeli.

I was saddened to learn that Mike Ginsberg's son Lt. Col. Eli Ginsberg had been killed Oct. 8 fighting the scores of Hamas invaders who were still in Kibbutz Be'eri the day after the attack began. (Photo provided by IDF).

»» ««

I vividly remember a moment at the end of my long-ago day with Mike Ginsberg. As night approached, I walked with him toward a terrace overlooking the great valley at the top of Israel's northern Galilee region. I asked him again if he ever thought of moving somewhere safer.

"Why would I?" he said. "I love my life."

It was a life of much risk and little comfort—not just terrorism but Israel's domestic challenges, such as high taxes, divisive politics and vexing questions about land, peace and war. But like many Israelis, perhaps even most, Mike felt he was part of something larger than himself. His life here gave him purpose, and a belief he was where he belonged.

As we stood on the overlook, Mike pointed to the view—the stunning Hula Valley and beyond it, the Golan Heights of Syria.

Often, we picture great things, and are disappointed when we see them, but as I stared now at this vista, it was just what I thought the land of the Bible would look like. The sky was magenta with a muted haze, and the haze suffused all the elements so that the valley and mountains became one. They became one with the sky, forming a magnificent realm. And it made me understand how this part of the world gave birth to faith. To look at this vista, this realm is to be in awe of any God who could create such majesty.

The effect is similar throughout Israel and the Palestinian territories. The land here gets a hold on you like few other places, and it won't let go. It gets a hold on you because it is beautiful and because it is difficult, forcing all who live here to sacrifice important things to make a home in it. And if your heritage was born here, and your prophets walked here, and your brethren died here, and maybe even your children, how can you ever let go of this land? How?

Adnan Husseini, a prominent architect who became Palestinian governor of East Jerusalem, welcomed me in 1991 to his home on the West Bank, where his family has roots going back 800 years. He pointed to a Jewish settlement built nearby. "Who gave them the right to be here?" he asked. (Photo by Mark Patinkin)

FIFTEEN

ARAB AND JEW ON
THE WEST BANK

Since Oct. 7, the world has fixated on what brought Jews and Arabs to this difficult quarrel.

The shorthand Palestinian argument is that the Jews are on their land.

A Jewish cab driver gave me the Israeli argument: "They make a war, they lose, they want everything back. Arabs should know, if you make a war, you can lose, not only win."

In essence, two peoples claim the same territory.

Jews will tell you they've yearned for it since the Romans pushed them from Israel, 2,000 years ago. Over time, under Crusaders,

Muslims, Ottomans, and the British, Palestine saw Arabs from neighboring countries like Egypt set roots here.

But Jews never left, and many who did held onto a dream of return. By 1900, in Europe, it was given a name, Zionism, after Mount Zion, a Jerusalem hilltop just outside the Old City. The movement's vision: re-create the biblical Jewish nation as a refuge from global anti-Semitism. By the 1930s, hundreds of thousands of Jews joined those who'd been here for centuries, angering many Palestinians.

At last, after the Nazi Holocaust, the world acted—but not just for Jews. In 1947 the United Nations carved British-mandate Palestine in half, creating two nations. The one for Jews was called Israel; the one for Arabs would be Palestine.

But the Palestinians said no. Why should these newcomers, these alien Jews, get half the land we claim? Six neighbor Arab states agreed, and in 1948, unleashed the first Arab-Israeli war. Israelis insist most Palestinians left their homes willingly so the Arab armies could sweep in. Arabs say they were driven out by the Jews. The truth is that both things happened, and Palestinians ended up in refugee camps in Gaza and the West Bank.

At first, they weren't Israel's problem. For 19 years after 1948, Gaza was under Egypt; the West Bank, Jordan. That changed with the Six-Day War of 1967, when Israel overran both territories. They occupied Gaza until 2005, and the West Bank still.

Palestinians are often stereotyped as resentful souls in refugee camps. It is true for some, but as I learned being among them, it is hardly all, or even most.

Which brings me to the first of two profiles in this chapter.

I give you Adnan Husseini, 44 when I met him in 1991, and 77 today.

He's an architect, politician and a man of grace and vision. He was waiting to greet me 33 years ago as I walked the stone steps to his entry door in Palestinian territory a few miles east of Jerusalem.

Getting there hadn't been easy. Jewish cab drivers weren't game to take me. The West Bank? Hadn't I heard of the intifada? It wasn't worth a rock through the windshield. So I tried cabs on Jerusalem's Arab side, but they said my timing was bad—a Palestinian strike had been called. If you work on a day like that, you risk being labeled a collaborator. So I upped the fare, offering $200, double the rate for a half-day's work, prompting the driver to smile and open his back door for me—"Please." It's how the Middle East works; anything for the right price.

Soon, I arrived at Adnan Husseini's home in a hilly, upscale area not far from Ramallah.

"Welcome," he said.

Adnan had thinning hair, a gentle manner, and was dressed casually in a short-sleeved button-up shirt. As we sat on his stone porch, one of his young daughters came out and crawled onto her father's lap.

"This is Majit," he said. He tried to coax her to say hello, but she played shy. She was in a jealous phase, Adnan explained; she liked her father for herself.

It was a beautiful, prosperous home in a nice area, close enough to Jerusalem but with breathing room and a great view. Adnan motioned toward the vista around us—a necklace of old Arabic villages. Then he pointed to a distant hamlet that stood out differently, newer and more geometrical, like a planned community.

"Givat Ze'ev," he said. A Jewish settlement. Like most, it was on the top of a hill. It was founded on an abandoned Jordanian military camp around 15 years before. But Palestinians feel such land should be theirs.

"Who gave them the right to be here?" Adnan said. "It is only the right of force." But it wasn't spoken in anger, just melancholy.

From his ancestral West Bank home, Adnan Husseini watched the emergence of a Jewish settlement called Givat Ze'ev, founded in 1977, with a new section of homes shown here in 2010, its population today approaching 20,000. (Photo by Debbie Hill).

I turned to his daughter and asked if she knew who built that village.

She giggled.

Did she think Jewish settlers?

She nodded.

I asked if it was okay for Jewish families to live there?

"Yes, why not? If they are nice."

Was it all right for Jewish houses to keep going up?

She burrowed into her father's chest and kept smiling. It seemed a game to her.

"Not good," she said.

Her father watched her answers curiously. It was clear he had seldom heard her address such issues.

I asked what kind of play she likes. Dolls?

"Too many dolls," said her father. And he worried she watched too much TV.

Her dream?

To have her own country of Palestine, she told me.

"I want to live like the others," Majit said.

Like children everywhere, said her father.

I asked Adnan how long his family had lived here, an important question in a struggle where both sides insist their roots go deepest.

He smiled at this.

"A long time," he said. I prodded him for a number.

The Husseini family, he said, had been in and around Jerusalem for 800 years. At that, he went inside, then emerged with an elaborate family tree, the names inscribed on 1,000 artistically drawn leaves. Toward the top of it was the name of Abraham himself.

"I thought Abraham was considered the father of Judaism," I said.

He is also one of the most revered of all Muslim figures, Adnan told me.

"He is our common grandfather." Indeed, he said Jews and Palestinians should be brothers.

"So why is there so much trouble in the family?"

He laughed at that. "Ordinary trouble between relations."

Then he grew serious. Over the centuries, conquerors had persecuted both Jews and Arabs on this land they share. It is a shame, he said, that victims of common enemies were now enemies themselves.

How, I asked, did it come to that?

"The Jews, they no longer want us here."

I noticed an elegant pen in his shirt pocket. Another daughter peeked through the front door. She was wearing a T-shirt printed with teddy bears and candy canes.

In Gaza, it seemed that poverty made many Palestinians dream constantly of a homeland. I wondered if those who were comfortable felt less yearning.

"Life seems good for you," I told him.

Yes, Adnan said, he was eating well with his family, but that was not enough.

"I also need to live in dignity."

What would give him that?

He told me of watching the last Olympics on television and remembered a difficult moment: the opening parade. He recalled his eyes filling up as each team went by, proudly waving their national flag. But there was none for Palestine.

"It made me very sad," he said. One of the hardest of all things, he told me, was to be part of a flagless people. To feel dignity, that is what he needed—a flag of his recognized nation.

As an Arab, didn't he feel he could embrace the flags of many of the 20 Arab countries?

"We are not wanted there," Adnan said. There was only one place his people could ever belong—a land of their own right here. He added that the Jews should understand what that is like.

I asked if the footprint of the settlers was really a threat. At the time that Adnan and I talked, there were 100,000 settlers among more than a million West Bank Palestinians.

"When I drive from Jerusalem to here," he said, "I see more each day. It is a feeling that they are slowly surrounding us."

The West Bank, he told me, is not a big territory. "We will soon have no place to live. No place to breathe."

Indeed, today, 33 years later, there are almost 700,000 Jews on the West Bank among three million Palestinians, the Jewish percentage of the population rising.

As for Givat Ze'ev, the nearby Jewish settlement Adnan had pointed out to me, it has grown from a population of perhaps 5,000 in 1991 to 20,000 today.

Adnan asked if I wanted coffee. I told him no need to bother, but he insisted on bringing me a cup. As I'd learned, hospitality is everything to Palestinians.

I asked him to give another example of not being able to live in dignity.

He said he has a grown daughter, born in Jerusalem, who wants to move there now but can't.

Why not?

"She needs permission."

From whom?

"The Israeli authorities." It is the same for him, and he refers now to Israel's prime minister at that time, Yitzhak Shamir.

"I am here 800 years, before Shamir set foot here, and I must get permission from him to live in my own land. This is hard."

It is also hard, he said, to be without citizenship. There are things all peoples like to aspire to, he told me—like serving in their own national Parliament, a realistic goal for a prominent figure like Adnan Husseini. But Palestinians cannot dream such dreams.

He spoke of his son, 16. "This morning," he said, "he left here to get an application to the University of Bethlehem, and I am nervous."

Why?

"He is a good boy, but if there is trouble anywhere nearby, they would close an area and make arrests, and it could be him."

I heard the same in 2024 from many I spoke to on the West Bank.

Adnan's two young daughters climbed onto his lap as he talked about his son. Adnan was proud of him, telling me the boy had just finished high school with excellent grades.

"And now I want him to leave the country."

Why?

The fear of random arrest, he said. "I don't want him to lose his future."

I pivoted to ask what he wanted for a homeland. I expected him to claim what those in Gaza did: most of Israel itself. But he didn't. He pictured a Palestinian nation in the West Bank and Gaza, side by side with Israel.

For peace to work, Adnan Husseini said, you can't have the

whole dream. There must be willingness for both Jews and Palestinians to give up some of it.

I turned the topic to terrorism. Jews, I said, are afraid a Palestinian state will be a launching base for attackers.

"If we have our own state, there would be no reason for that. It will stop the hatred."

What of the extremists whose goal is to destroy Israel—who won't settle for just the West Bank and Gaza?

"Give us a government and we would take care of them," said Husseini. "We cannot now."

What about the Jewish settlers? Would he insist that they leave?

"We must be pragmatic now," he said. "They are here. We are on the land together. We should live together."

As he spoke, his eyes fell on Givat Ze'ev, the nearby Jewish settlement.

"If you want everything," he said, "you will have nothing." He added that it is a thought for Israel, too.

"I am not saying to Jews, 'You don't belong here,'" said Adnan. "I am saying, 'I do belong here.'"

Before I left, he gave me a tour of his house, showing me a photo of his grandfather in Jerusalem as well as centuries-old furniture from his forebears—artifacts of deep roots.

I asked if he sleeps well these days.

Sleep, Adnan said, is not just to close your eyes. It is to have a satisfied heart. And he did not feel he would have this until he lies down at night in his own nation.

>> «<

Hoping to reconnect with Adnan Husseini in 2024, I search online to see how his life has unfolded, and learn he's had an impressive journey. Now 77, he was Palestinian governor of Jerusalem from 2008 to 2018, and until recently remained active in Jerusalem affairs for the Palestinian Authority.

In 2005, he hosted U.S. first lady Laura Bush on a tour of the sacred Dome of the Rock mosque on the Temple Mount.

But his roles also drew him into the area's contentious issues. A number of times, Husseini criticized Israel for taking over Arab homes in East Jerusalem to expand the Jewish presence there. That's a volatile topic since Palestinians demand that side of the city as their capital in a two-state solution. A few times, he was at vocal odds with Israel around similar controversies, and in part because of that, in 2018, he had his passport confiscated and was barred from attending a UN conference in Lebanon. For me, that was an insight into the indignities even moderate Palestinian figures sometimes face.

In another prestigious posting, Husseini was a supervisor of the Waqf, which oversees the 37-acre Temple Mount whose Dome of the Rock forms Jerusalem's signature image. Several times, he called out Israel for closing access to it for Muslims after various incidents there. Collective punishment, he said.

For officials like Adnan Husseini, one's public image is often shaped by quotes around news events. But he's much more than that. If you search more deeply, you'll find he has been on many charitable boards, was named to promote West Bank tourism and is a standout part of his community's fabric. Earlier in his career as an architect, he helped renovate the Al-Aqsa Mosque itself.

He is seen today as a prominent Palestinian figure, an elder statesman with an accomplished life.

I was also impressed to see the journey of the 16-year-old son he mentioned when I visited. Back then, Adnan was worried his boy could be targeted on the West Bank simply for being young, male and Palestinian. But the son ended up going to college in America and is now a highly regarded professor of Chemical and Biological Engineering in the United Arab Emirates with a recent patent for an improved way of delivering chemotherapy with fewer side effects.

I managed to find Adnan Husseini's contact information, and

in 2024, reached out to him to catch up. I did not hear back. I sent emails and left several voice and text messages on his phone—definitely the right number since his face populated the WhatsApp listing. But no luck.

I was disappointed but understood. Perhaps he simply wants to avoid the spotlight—and inevitable questions about politics—during this volatile time.

A time when the dreams he spoke of in 1991—of Palestinian self-determination and peace—are further away than ever.

One can only wish those two things for his people.

And for Adnan Husseini, a sound sleep and satisfied heart.

»» ««

Although I failed to reconnect with Husseini, I did manage to reach another West Bank dweller I'd visited during that same 1991 trip—a Jewish settler named Yisrael Medad.

There's a reason I'm profiling him and Husseini here—it's worth stating again that the West Bank, even more than Gaza, will foretell the future of the Israeli-Palestinian challenge.

Medad is 76 today, but let's start with when I met him at age 44. He lived in Shiloh, a citadel of homes perched on a hill by empty land an hour from Jerusalem.

It was much further into the West Bank than the home of Adnan Husseini. To get to Shiloh, my cab had to wind through Arab villages as well as Jewish settlements that were easy to spot—new houses carved into hilltops like circled wagon trains. At one point, my Arab driver put on his right turning signal and left it blinking for three minutes. "A bad section," he said. The signal, he explained, was code that our car was Palestinian.

We passed steep, rocky hills terraced over the centuries and planted with olive trees, some so old they're said to date to Christ.

Finally, we were at Shiloh.

Yisrael Medad, posed for me in 1991 with his wife Beth and daughter Tzruya in Shiloh, a Jewish settlement that predates the first temple. "We consider this part of Israel," said Medad. "We are back on our land." (Photo by Mark Patinkin)

Medad, in yarmulke, welcomed me into his stucco home. At the time, 1991, he was one of only 700 residents. He worked as a staffer for an Israeli right-wing party, commuting an hour to Jerusalem.

Medad grew up in Queens, his father managing a women's garment factory.

"The shmata trade," he told me—Yiddish for "rags" or clothing. Medad's Zionism deepened at a Yeshiva high school in Forest Hills. After work in London connecting young folks to Israel, Medad "made Aliyah"—Hebrew for ascending—moving to Jerusalem in 1970 with his new wife Beth. He was 28, she 26. For a while, the two lived in the Jewish quarter of the Old City, and then, in 1981, became settlers on the West Bank. As early Shiloh pioneers, they started in a mobile shelter, five years later building the home where I found them.

I asked why, as Jews, they would put down roots in a territory many fear to even visit.

New York, he said—now that was dangerous; Shiloh wasn't so bad.

"My 8- and 10-year-old are off playing right now, and I don't know where," Beth told me. "They just said, 'We're going off to see who's home.' Sometimes, they're gone for six hours. Can you do that in America?"

I pointed out that children can play freely inside Israel.

"We consider this part of Israel," said Medad. "We are back on our land."

Why does he see it that way?

Yisrael Medad told me Jews were in Shiloh on the West Bank–Samaria as he calls it–hundreds of years before Solomon built the first temple in Jerusalem. He sent me this photo of him and his wife Beth standing by a nearby 3,500-year-old stone wall.

It's in the Bible—Joshua founded the first kingdom of the Jews in Shiloh over 3,000 years ago, centuries before King David's son Solomon built the first temple in Jerusalem. In fact, Medad pointed out, Shiloh was home to the tabernacle that housed the Ark of the Covenant containing the tablets of Moses. He later sent me a photo of him and his wife Beth by a nearby 3,500-year-old stone wall. There was a second reason he moved to what he calls Samaria.

"Wherever you went you ran against barbed wire," he said of his country's borders. "You felt claustrophobic."

So he was also here to bolster Israel's security, explaining that settlements add a Jewish footprint and buffer on the West Bank. Many Israelis disagree with that, saying settlers are cowboys who ratchet up tensions. But the Medads say it's as natural for Jews to be here as for longtime Arab-Israelis to live in Israel.

Beth, 40, served coffee cake as we sat at the kitchen table. They were raising three daughters and two sons in Shiloh. I asked if it's fair to impose their politics of settlement on their kids.

"I think it's made my children stronger," said Beth. "Living out here, arguing with other Israelis about it—and unfortunately having rocks thrown. But even that's made them stronger."

Their 18-year-old daughter, Tzruya, came into the room. I asked if she liked Shiloh.

Very much—her neighbors are terrific. Then she laughed. "As a teenager, it's not the best place to be. It's away from all the action."

Has she had rocks thrown at her?

"Yes, sure." Sometimes none for months, sometimes three times a week. But it's better now that they've put hard plastic over the school bus windows. Of course, she added, Molotovs can be more dangerous.

"My wife had one on Hanukkah," said Medad. "Last December." It ricocheted off the car and splashed flames on the highway. Another Molotov, he said, went through a neighbor's windshield, covering everyone with gasoline, but there was no ignition.

"The miracle rate here," he said, "is high."

I asked if he had a gun.

"An M-16." A military assault rifle.

For what?

Medad shared in guard duty here. He also had a 9mm pistol he often carried when commuting to work in Jerusalem. The route went past three refugee camps. A number of times, youths had thrown stones at his car. When that happens, Medad stops and chases them on foot.

"If you don't, they end up throwing stones at the next Jewish car—maybe a woman inside."

Settlers, he explained, aren't prone to turn a cheek; they are no longer ghetto Jews.

"This is our own country," said Medad.

They gave me a tour of their house. There were posters of Bruce Springsteen and Madonna in a daughter's room, and I wondered if the ancient prophets of Shiloh imagined their descendants worshiping such idols.

Back in the kitchen, a well-fed cat stood by a window overlooking the valley below. As we took in the view, I asked if the creation of Shiloh pushed Arabs off their property.

"Look around," said Medad. "This was empty land." He insisted it was un-deeded. And that the rocky hill Shiloh was built upon was a difficult place to homestead.

"I'd love to have put all this down in the valley," he said of his village, "but we decided to only live where no Arab would think of living."

So why are Palestinians angry that you're here?

"They don't want Jews to be seen or heard of."

I was surprised that 40 percent of Shiloh's residents have jobs in the settlement itself. Beth explained most were involved in children's programs and schools.

"It's like the old Gerber commercial," she said. "Babies are our business. Our only business."

There are a lot of babies here?

She smiled. "Anything under four kids is a medical problem."

As Beth offered more coffee cake, I asked what they will do if there's a two-state solution with a Palestinian homeland on the West Bank.

Medad couldn't imagine it would happen. "This is our country."

And if it does happen?

"Many people," he told me, "would decide to remain behind and live here. I would. Shiloh was the center of Jewish life when Jerusalem was still a backwater, and you're going to tell me Jews don't have a right to be here?"

Beth said her family is no different from pioneers in other countries.

Shiloh, now a modern Jewish settlement deep in the West Bank, was an ancient Jewish city in biblical Samaria.

"Where were those American wagon trains going?" she said, then answered: To make sure future generations would have a secure nation.

Does that mean she wanted to push Palestinians off the West Bank?

No—but millions of Israeli-Arabs live among Jews in Israel. Why can't Jews live here among Arabs?

Later, I looked up Shiloh in the Bible.

I was struck by what Joshua told the Israelites as he declared Shiloh a center of their new kingdom.

"How much longer," he said, "will you neglect to take possession of the land which the Lord the God of our fathers has given you?"

And so the Israelites did, until the Romans drove them out, and now the family of Yisrael Medad, from Queens, has returned, making a stand among Palestinians.

Before I left, they invited me to a ceremony just starting at Shiloh's temple—the ritual circumcision of a baby boy. The temple was a mobile home. Afterward, I stood among 50 people in the sun, and all around, there was a mood of great joy. A new infant had been consecrated into the faith. Far below us, in the center of the valley, an Arab shepherd tended his herd.

>»» «««

And now, in 2024, I'm about to connect with Yisrael Medad again. It was not hard to track him down—he occasionally writes op-eds for the *Jerusalem Post*, which lists his email. After arranging a call time, I dial Medad's number, and when he answers, he tells me he's speaking from the same home where we'd shared an afternoon 33 years before.

His teenage kids have since given him grandchildren; he had just returned from visiting them in Jerusalem. Medad was about to mark his 43rd year in Shiloh—a reminder of how long settlers have been in the West Bank, the first having arrived 57 years ago after the war of 1967.

Shiloh's population of 700 from when I was there has grown to 3,000—but including neighboring settlements that have been established nearby, it's 10,000.

I presume by now Shiloh would have built a security fence, like almost all other 144 West Bank settlements. They haven't.

"We're ideologically opposed to fences," Medad tells me.

You are?

"We do not want to live in a ghetto. And fences are usually broken into sooner or later." They prefer to focus on electronic security.

Has Shiloh been targeted?

Thankfully no, says Medad, but three years ago, two Jewish teenagers were shot by a Palestinian extremist at a nearby bus stop.

I ask how Shiloh folks are regarded these days. As radical settlers?

"I wouldn't call myself radical. I guess the *New York Times* would probably describe me that way."

Medad today sees Shiloh residents as he did back then—they have a right to live near their biblical roots. To bar Jews from their ancestral lands for being Jews, he says, would be apartheid.

His wife Beth is now a retired English teacher. As for the daughter with the Springsteen and Madonna posters, she's a lawyer with four children living in a nearby settlement of 3,000 called Ofra.

Their other four kids live in Jerusalem.

"Not the West Bank?" I ask, then catch myself. "Do you call it the West Bank?"

Never. To Medad, it's biblical Judea and Samaria.

Shiloh's economy has expanded into wine making on some of the world's oldest vineyard grounds. They also have computer start-ups and an olive production operation.

Do many Arabs work in Shiloh's businesses?

They used to, Medad says—until Oct. 7.

Before that, there were dozens in Shiloh companies and another 150 Palestinians doing construction there. No more, and without them, many new houses and buildings are on hold.

As in every Israeli community, they've been touched by the war. One young soldier from Shiloh was killed in Gaza. Another man was kidnapped on Oct. 7. He was in a well-known video from that day, the one showing a half-Chinese Jewish woman named Noa Argamani, 26, crying "Don't kill me," as she was brutally driven away from the Nova festival on a motorcycle.

Noa was sandwiched between two members of a civilian mob who followed Hamas into Israel to join in the havoc. The view in that video then swings to Noa's boyfriend, a tall man in a gray shirt, hands tied, eyes grim, being shoved forward by three shouting militants.

His name is Avinatan Or, age 30, the second of seven brothers and an electrical engineering graduate of Ben Gurion University in Be'er Sheva.

He grew up in Shiloh.

"I know the family," says Medad. "I know the mother." It has been a terrible ordeal for them.

In early June of 2024, Noa Argamani was among four Israeli hostages rescued out of Gaza in an IDF raid. But Avinatan Or of Shiloh is still being held.

I am speaking to Medad six months after the war started. I ask what Israel should do now.

"I just know Hamas cannot be left in any position of power," he says, "whether civilian, political or military." As Jihadists, he feels they will never stop trying to make war and kill Jews.

What would he say to those who accuse Israel of genocide?

He mentions the Holocaust, where six million died, and says: "I don't think they know the definition of it. I don't pay too much attention."

Is he disturbed by pro-Palestinian sentiment on U.S. campuses?

"I have close to 60 years of political activism myself," says Medad, "and have participated in sit-ins. But these demonstrations are low-level terrorism. They're trying to drive fear into Jews more than getting a policy implemented."

I wonder if the war has made things on the West Bank, where tensions are now high, more difficult for Medad.

Not really.

"I take buses that are all bullet proof," he says. "I feel relaxed traveling from Shiloh to Jerusalem."

As for his career, a decade after I saw him in 1991, Medad began doing educational programming at the Menachem Begin Heritage Center in Jerusalem. Begin, Israel's sixth prime minister, was a member of the militant Zionist group Irgun that fought the British before 1948 when they occupied Palestine by mandate. In 1978, Begin made peace with Egypt. But he also founded the right-wing Likud party, which Israel's controversial prime minister, Benjamin Netanyahu, now leads.

Although retired, Medad is still active as a Menachem Begin fellow. In a recent published commentary, he lamented that Jews around the world now worry that wearing Jewish symbols or even going to temple will make them targets of people calling them war criminals.

"The worst, I fear, is yet to come," Medad wrote.

Does he feel a Palestinian state would create peace?

No. Medad is against a two-state solution.

"Within two days," he says, "or two weeks, the missiles would start." Just as happened in Gaza soon after Israel withdrew in 2005.

But isn't the Palestinian Authority more moderate than Hamas?

"The PA is still paying the families of Palestinian terrorists in jail," he says. "It's pay for slay. You get so much for injuring Jews, and more for killing them." He paused and said, "That's still ongoing."

But isn't the PA still preferable to Hamas?

"Definitely Hamas would take over here just like they did in 2006 in Gaza," he tells me, "and we're back where we started from."

But aren't Jewish settlements in Palestinian territory an obstacle to peace?

When I reconnected with Yisrael Medad in 2024, he told me he and his wife Beth were still in the same home in Shiloh, and sent me this current photo. When I pointed out that some say the West Bank's almost 700,000 Jewish settlers should leave, Medad asked—does that mean the 2 million Israeli-Arabs should leave Israel?

"If that's the case," says Medad, "should Israel throw all the Israeli-Arabs out?"

That would be two million people.

"Let's call Nazareth," Medad says, referring to Israel's biggest Arab city, population 80,000. "Ask them, 'Do you want to take all the Jews out of Judea and Samaria, and we'll take all the Arabs out of Israel? Would that be an adequate quid pro quo?' Their answer would be, 'No.'"

He pauses and adds: "Jews should be able to live where they want to live. Just like everyone else."

I ask how he looks back on his life in Israel.

He feels his role in recreating Shiloh has continued a chain of

Jewish history begun with Abraham and the children of Moses. And his example has inspired others to put their own roots in what he calls the ancestral Jewish ground of Judea and Samaria.

"When we came here, the land around us was empty," says Medad. Now, from this high ground, he sees many other Jewish settlements.

Palestinians I met on my 2024 trip, like Omar who showed me Bethlehem, consider it encroachment—Jews taking up more and more of the Palestinian West Bank. As Omar put it, "Shway, shway." Little bit, little bit.

Medad sees it differently. It was empty ground, he insists. And besides, it's Jews returning to their lineal home, bequeathed unto them by both history and the Bible itself.

One can argue they're both right.

Or not

But they are both there, each sinking roots against the odds in this beautiful, difficult land, Arab and Jew side by side.

As I say goodbye on the phone to Yisrael Medad, I find myself thinking again what I'd thought early on during this journey.

There has to be a way.

I spent a morning in an Arab souk in Jaffa near Tel Aviv seeking those with family in Gaza. But most Israeli-Arabs preferred not to talk about the war, worried how Israeli authorities would react if they criticized it, and how Palestinians would if they didn't. (Photo by Robby Berman)

SIXTEEN

TRYING TO SEE THE WAR

I feel it's important during this 2024 trip to see the war itself. Since international journalists aren't allowed to enter Gaza on our own, there is one other option—embedding with the Israeli military. Critics will say that's a managed show, but it's how reporters cover many conflicts, and our role is to witness however we can.

I learn quickly the odds are long.

The North American Media Desk of the IDF says they'll put me on a list but can't promise. Such trips don't happen often, and when they do, seats in the Humvees are limited.

As my days here go by, I start to pull as many strings as I can.

The guide I hired knows a retired general and can have him call for me. I ask other contacts to put in a word through their connections. Mostly, I message the IDF media people every day. You need to stay on their radar.

Finally, a week in, I receive a WhatsApp text saying there could be a Gaza embed the next morning. But hours later, it's bumped a day, and another, and then nothing happens. The war is like that. The IDF has other things to worry about besides reporters.

My push to get inside Gaza isn't the trip's only challenge.

I arrived in Israel 100 days after Oct. 7, and learned this can be an emotional breakpoint for those affected. A lot has been made of that milestone here, reminding everyone of how much they've been through.

The land of Israel–as well as Gaza to the south–is blessed with a beautiful Mediterranean waterfront. On a sunny, breezy day in Jaffa, I paused to take in the vista. (Photo by Robby Berman)

One example: Several hostage families I asked for interviews decide at the last minute that they're emotionally not able. Setting up a visit to a destroyed Kibbutz was hard, too. Understandably, they want it done with dignity, with survivors offering a limited number of tours each day. It took a week to be granted a spot.

Other plans simply don't work out. It's a risk of journeying to a place in upheaval and trying to find your way. One idea was to talk to Israeli Arabs with family in Gaza. How was the war impacting them? I was told to look in Jaffa where, in one of the earliest moments of Christianity, the apostle Peter received a vision from God.

During the 1948 war, 120,000 Arabs fled from Jaffa to Gaza, a mere 3,900 remaining. Today, there are 16,000 Jaffa Arabs out of a population of 52,000. Might some of those Arab families still have relatives in Gaza?

I went to find out, walking through souks to ask. But 76 years is a long time, and unlike the West Bank and Gaza, where people cling to 1948 like it was yesterday, here, they seem to have moved on. That's typical of many Israeli-Arabs, and makes you wonder how different things might have been had millions of Palestinians not been kept to this day in refugee status by the United Nations.

Even Mahmoud had moved on.

I find him in a Jaffa flea market selling everything from old vases to burnt pans. He's in his 60s and had what I was looking for—brothers and sisters in Gaza. Interestingly, they chose to move there from Israel just a few decades ago, as did Mahmoud himself to run a business, but he came back. Yet he told me he hadn't talked to his Gazan family in a year or two.

Is he afraid for them now? Angry about the war?

Everything, Mahmoud says simply, is part of Allah's greater plan.

I ask if it's hard to be an Israeli-Arab.

"As long as you are good," Mahmoud says, "you are treated well."

And how is it compared to his years in Gaza?

After a long day in Ramallah, I had to leave the bus at the West Bank border and go through a checkpoint before catching a second bus on the Israeli side back to Jerusalem. (Photo by Mark Patinkin)

"Life is better here."

Politely, he adds that's all he'd like to say about it—were there any items he could sell me?

When I approach others in the souk saying I am a journalist, they don't want to talk, either. For many, it's delicate. They worry how Israeli authorities will react if they criticize the war, and how Palestinians will if they don't.

Of course, some in Jaffa have indeed lost loved ones in Gaza, but I didn't come across them that afternoon.

Yet as long as you get out in the field, you'll often come across something worthy. I moved on that day to Hostage Square in nearby Tel Aviv, where I had poignant interviews with parents of the taken.

For my first day in Israel, I was here with a Rhode Island mission, but the weeks since have been on my own. Some of those nights have been lonely, in part because I was sending back live dispatches every day, leaving little time to take breaks with those I'd begun to connect with. You need to reserve your evenings to write.

That schedule also made for periods of exhaustion, like a long, two-bus dance one evening coming back late from the West Bank, writing in my seat, getting off at a checkpoint, then waiting in the dark for a second bus to Jerusalem. Just after I boarded that one, I got messages that my next day's plans had fallen through—in that case, a planned interview with the mother of a hostage.

That can take a mental toll, putting thoughts of failure in your head. I've had many low moments around that. Self-doubt is a stressful companion. This is not the kind of trip you want to take if you're going through a bad time.

But now, with only days left here, a WhatsApp message has just arrived. It's from Noa, the IDF media contact I've been texting.

A journalist's trip into Gaza is on for the next morning, and I've been granted a space in the Humvee. Noa gives me the location of a deployment spot to meet just outside the border, two hours from Jerusalem, where I'm staying.

But I have to find my own helmet and bulletproof vest, and with the trip called for the next morning, I need to scramble.

I spend hours on the phone, as does my guide Robby, but no luck—such gear is in demand. Then I try a Jerusalem journalist named Lazar Berman who's from my home state of Rhode Island. He had emailed me before I left for the Middle East.

I was told I'd need my own bulletproof gear to go into Gaza with the IDF, and on short notice was lucky to find a set from an Israeli journalist named Lazar Berman who grew up near me in Providence.

"Been reading you my entire life," he said of my Providence Journal column. "My brother in Pawtucket saw you were heading to Israel to cover the war. Happy to assist." Small world.

Lazar grew up blocks from me and is now diplomatic correspondent for the *Times of Israel*. Only weeks before, he'd been in Gaza himself as a reserve soldier and was happy to lend me his Army helmet, as well as a "PRESS" vest from his paper.

He lived a mile from my hotel—I told him I'd take the light rail.

"It's heavy," Lazar texted of the gear, "you'll want to cab." He was right.

Lazar had to work late, so it wasn't until 10:30 p.m. the night before that we linked up outside his apartment building.

But the IDF doesn't commit to a trip until it starts. Their text had only said, "Keep your calendar clear for 10:30 a.m. at the Ein HaShlosha area." That's a Kibbutz near Gaza where a half dozen were murdered Oct. 7, with an Army base now nearby."

As I go to bed at 1 a.m., I'm still expecting it to be canceled—a hard rain is forecast.

But when I wake up at 5:30 a.m., it's confirmed.

Within hours, I will be inside Gaza.

Rotem Mathias, 16, survived Oct. 7 lying between a household bed and wall with his mom, Deborah, draped over him. She was murdered, but the Hamas invaders didn't see Rotem beneath her. I met Rotem in the home of his uncle, Aron Troen, who has taken him into his family. (Photo by Mark Patinkin)

SEVENTEEN

"MOM AND DAD R DEAD"

Except for an occasional Facebook message, I had not connected with my old high school friend Michael since we graduated many decades ago.

But not long after Oct. 7, as I sat in my home office in Providence, I got a message from him.

"My niece and her husband were murdered," it said.

Just that. No other words. It was clear he wrote in part because I'm a journalist. And so I called him.

The name of Michael's niece was Debbie Mathias. She was 50 and born in the states but lived with her husband Shlomi, 47, in a small Israeli kibbutz called Holit, a mile from Gaza. The two were peaceniks, the kind who marched for a two-state solution and had a "Palestinian Lives Matter" pin in their home. Shlomi taught music at a mixed Arab and Jewish high school. Debbie had long brown hair and looked younger than her years. Both did, really. You could tell from their photos it was from living a happy life.

When the Oct. 7 assault began, they went to join their 16-year-old son Rotem in his bedroom, which had been reinforced as the home's secure area. That is what Rotem woke up to. Soon after, militants were inside the house. Shlomi, the father, along with Rotem, tried to barricade the bedroom door with a mattress. There were a few minutes of struggle. One can only imagine the fear. Then the attackers forced the door open and threw in a hand grenade. Shlomi took the impact of it. The last words he was heard to say were, "I've lost my arm." By then, Debbie had draped herself over their son Rotem in the narrow space between a bed and the wall.

The room filled with smoke and dust from the explosion, as well as from a couch that had been set on fire in the house. The Hamas men then came in. There was chaotic gunfire as they sought to kill whoever was inside. They left Shlomi to bleed to death, then saw Debbie and shot her at close range, ending her life. One of the bullets went through the bed and struck Rotem in the stomach. He managed to remain quiet and somehow, they didn't see him.

For the next 10 hours, Rotem hid as the killers came back into the house more than once. Almost impossibly, he survived.

"You know," my friend Michael told me, "miracles."

»» ««

The two of us went to high school together on the south side of Chicago. Michael now lives with his wife in Portland, Oregon. I'll explain in a moment why I'm only using his first name, though he was willing to have it published. It has to do with the fear many American Jews have felt since Oct. 7.

Michael's murdered niece was the daughter of his older sister Carol Troen. She lives in Israel with her husband Ilan Troen, who grew up in Boston. At age 83, Ilan is still a prominent Israel Studies academic both at Brandeis and Ben Gurion University in Be'er Sheva, not far from where the killings took place. He and Carol had six children.

"Now they have five," said Michael.

A day after his daughter Debbie was murdered, Ilan wrote an article about it posted by CNN. In it, Ilan said that in 1919, his own grandmother was killed in a pogrom in her Polish village of Rivne, today part of Ukraine. That, he wrote, was during a period that saw an astonishing 150,000 Jews slaughtered in such rampages.

"It is now my daughter who was brutally murdered," he said.

It happened the same way—attackers in 2023 killing Jews in their homes and villages just as happened in 1919.

Carol and Ilan's son Aron Troen, now 56, has taken his nephew Rotem into his family. Israel's Social Services Ministry says he was among 31 young people under age 25 orphaned that day, with an additional 250 minors losing one parent.

For the last 13 years, Aron has been a professor of nutrition science at the Hebrew University of Jerusalem. For the 23 years before that, he was at Tufts outside Boston.

Aron's home is in a suburban community between Tel Aviv and Jerusalem called Mazkeret Batya. A week after arriving in Israel, on a Monday evening, I headed there hoping to talk to Rotem about what happened that day, though Aron cautioned his nephew might not be up to it.

It was evening when I knocked on their door, the day's last light fading to dusk.

»» ««

I remember my friend Michael well. He was a theater guy in high school. We were once in the same play together, "Dark of the

Moon," a mystical fable set in Appalachia. I had two lines, while Michael was a lead as the wrinkled "Conjur Man." We chuckled about it on our call.

"They put the makeup and the face lines on me because he was about a hundred years old," Michael said of his character. "Now when I look at myself in the mirror, I say, 'Yeah, there he is.'"

Michael remembered a moment between us during senior year.

"I told you I just met the girl I'm going to marry," he recalled. "You looked at me incredulous, like, 'I can't believe someone in my class just said that.'"

More than 50 years later, they're still married, with four adult kids. Soon after graduating college, Michael and his wife moved to Israel, where he worked in theater in the city of Haifa. When Michael was called up for the Lebanon war of 1982, his Army assignment was to help entertain the troops.

After 10 years there, in 1984, they returned permanently to the States, settling near his wife's sister in Portland, where Michael still runs his own consumer finance company.

I asked him to tell me about his niece Debbie.

"She was very much a free spirit," Michael said. She met her husband Shlomi in a Tel Aviv arts college where they both studied music, which remained a big part of their lives.

Michael found out about the murders a bit late. That's because he is now an Orthodox Jew, shutting down electronics on the Sabbath. When news of the massacre began to post in America late on Saturday, Oct. 7, he didn't see it.

On Sunday, Michael was in synagogue for the holiday of Simchat Torah, which marks the end of the cycle of torah readings. During the service, he heard others say that Israel had been attacked.

"They came across the border from Gaza," someone told him. "Do you have anyone near there?"

Yes, his niece Debbie's family, but Michael felt at most it was a small skirmish.

"I had no idea of the severity," he told me.

He was in Chicago at the time, staying with his son, daughter-in-law and their newborn. He walked back from temple into their apartment, where his wife was babysitting. She came to him sobbing.

Michael asked if Debbie and Shlomi were all right.

"They were murdered," his wife said. "They killed them."

The next few hours are a bit of a fog to Michael. They made calls to his sister Carol, Debbie's mother, in Israel, where it was 4 a.m., but of course, everyone was up. Still, it took many hours to get the details.

It is Jewish tradition to bury the dead within a day or two of passing, but the funerals for Debbie and Shlomi didn't take place for almost 10 days.

"They identified Shlomi's body," Michael explained, "but they hadn't identified Debbie yet."

I asked why.

"There are hundreds of bodies in cold storage that were burned or mutilated," Michael explained. High-caliber bullets, he told me, do unthinkable damage, and many of the victims were shot in the head at close range, often more than once. Some, he added were decapitated.

Michael attended the funeral by Zoom.

"The sobs and the children saying goodbye to their parents," he told me, "and Rotem saying goodbye to his mom who saved his life—it's such pain. I don't think they can conceive of when that pain is ever going to go away."

Hoping to write about how the family was coping in Israel, I messaged Michael's sister Carol—grandmother to Rotem, 16, who survived the attack. Even with my introduction from Michael, I wasn't sure if she'd be open to hearing from a reporter. But she thanked me for reaching out. Despite her grief, or perhaps because of it, Carol felt it was important for people to hear not just about Oct. 7, but what survivors have been going through in the months since.

"The effort in the aftermath to carry on," she wrote me, "is often left behind the scenes. Yet that mostly untold story is crucial."

So I reached out to Carol's son Aron, Rotem's uncle and now guardian. He told me Rotem has struggled. Aron was unsure if an interview with his nephew would work out. He asked that I be in touch when I got to Israel.

Soon after arriving, I texted him again.

"It's been a stormy week," Aron responded. "I'll broach it with Rotem tomorrow and get back to you."

Finally, many days into my trip, we picked an evening for me to come by. Aron was willing to be interviewed as the uncle, but couldn't promise Rotem would feel up to it. A half hour before arriving, I texted that I'd soon be there.

"He has said yes in principle," Aron responded, "but every day is a new day."

Their home is in a treed, suburban enclave. Aron welcomed me in, apologizing for things being unkempt. With both he and his wife working, their other two teens busy with school, and many appointments for Rotem, life had been hectic.

Aron and I sat on the living room couch. He's 56 and taught at Tufts in Boston for many years. That's where he met his wife Susan, a software engineer. Their family has been in Israel since 2010. Their son Rafi is 15 and daughter Gabriella 17. And now Rotem has joined the family.

Aron comes off as thoughtful, and deeply considerate—at the end of the night, he drove me an hour back to Jerusalem to save me cab fare.

I began by asking how he's handling the murder of his younger sister Debbie.

"It's still a state of disbelief," Aron said, but added that like many in Israel, he's had to make room in his mourning for the needs of the living.

He said of Rotem: "His whole world has been—I'm trying to

think of the word in English—destroyed, really. He lost his parents, his home; and his friends are dispersed around the country."

Rotem's kibbutz had 54 families. It was a simple, quiet life, and now, even small things remind Rotem of what he's lost—like having to worry about traffic when walking the dog.

Aron paused to say he was still unsure if we would be joined by Rotem, who was in his room upstairs.

"It's exceedingly difficult," Aron told me. Rotem, he said, has compared himself to the time "The Hulk" said, "My secret is I'm always angry." Though in Rotem's case, it's not a positive.

But Rotem had also shown strength, such as during a trip to America when he spoke to congresspeople, including a private meeting with Nancy Pelosi.

"But then he came back to the hotel room and collapsed and withdrew," said Aron. "You can't always be strong."

In some ways, it has gotten harder for Rotem.

"The reality and depression and guilt are settling in," Aron told me.

It comes out in different ways, such as Rotem lately referring to Aron as his guardian instead of his uncle. Therapists have said it's a way to distance himself. Trauma reactions are complicated.

Rotem's two older sisters, 21 and 19, survived that day hiding in separate kibbutz flats. Aron told me they are coping with trauma too, but have aged out of state help and have to remake their lives on their own.

"They are struggling," said Aron, describing them as broken yet resilient—like their country.

Aron's home is an hour by car from northern Gaza, but the Oct. 7 violence reached him directly—they had to go to their own household shelter because of Hamas rockets, two of which struck 100 meters away.

His wider family was impacted, too. Rotem's cousin, a young woman serving in the Army, was assigned to a Gaza base that was overrun by Hamas. By grace, she was on leave for shabbat the Saturday it happened. But friends of hers were murdered and others kidnapped. Later, a video would come out of four young women from that base in a room with bloodied faces surrounded by chaotic Hamas members taunting them.

"We are not post-trauma," Aron said. "It's still ongoing."

A half hour or so into our conversation, someone began coming down the stairs. It was Rotem. He had decided to join us.

»» ««

Shlomi and Deborah Mathias, parents of Rotem and believers in coexistence with Palestinians, were murdered when Hamas invaded their home Oct. 7.

He is taller than I expected—over six feet, but with the slightly self-conscious manner of a teen. He sat nearby on a couch and for a few minutes, we talked about his hobbies—video games and martial arts.

Then I asked how he is doing.

"I don't know," Rotem said.

There were some seconds of silence. Then he went on.

"I obviously have unresolved trauma. And I need a lot of therapy and things like that, so I guess I'm not doing that good."

I asked if it's hard for him to talk about that day.

"It's more that nobody wants to listen." It's uncomfortable for them, he said, and they worry Rotem doesn't want to be asked, so it's avoided.

"Some people can't talk about violence," Rotem explained.

"Can you talk about it to me?" I said.

"The story?"

"Yes."

"Sure."

He was awakened that day at 6 a.m. by rockets, which happened often, but never so many. Soon, the kibbutz WhatsApp group began exchanging messages about missiles in the area, and terrorists breaching the community fence. Then he and his family heard automatic weapons fire.

Rotem's room is the household shelter, with reinforced walls, so his parents joined him in it. They closed the door but couldn't lock it since shelters were designed for bombs, not invaders.

Later, Aron shared a long family text string happening in real time that day among the Troen family all over Israel. I'll integrate that here into Rotem's description of what happened.

At 7:24 a.m., Debbie texted the family chat, saying, "Someone knocked on our door." This was well into the rocket attack.

They ignored the knock, sensing it was something ominous. They hoped whoever it was would move on. Minutes later, Debbie texted again: "Sounds of gunfire surrounding our home. We don't know what is going on."

Three minutes after that, Debbie texted: "I'm worried for my girls, who are alone."

She meant Rotem's older sisters Shir, 21 and Shakked, 19, who were each sheltering alone during the attack in separate studio apartments that were part of the kibbutz's youth housing.

A relative in the group reported that the larger nearby town of Sderot had been infiltrated by attackers.

At 7:35 a.m., Debbie sent out an alarming text.

"It sounds like they broke our glass," she wrote. "The back door. Lots of shooting."

Ilan, the family patriarch, was on the text string as "Dad." At 7:38 a.m., he texted what any father might. Simply: "Lock all entrances."

At 7:41 a.m, Debbie responded, "We did before entering the mamad." That's the security room. "But we are really scared."

A minute later she texted: "And someone can kick down our front door and the back door is just glass. Definitely a lot of shooting in the kibbutz."

Abie Troen, a documentary maker who is Debbie and Aron's youngest brother, texted at 7:44 a.m., "Please be strong and safe."

Another in the family added simply: "Praying."

That's when Debbie stopped texting.

The next message from Debbie's household—from Rotem — came 16 minutes later, at 8am. The murders of Debbie and Shlomi took place during that period.

As I spoke with Rotem, he told me how it happened. There was a thick, spare mattress in the room that he and his father dragged over to barricade the door.

The attackers, in the house now, began shouting "Allahu akbar." Debbie told Rotem to lie between the bed and the wall. Everything was happening fast. It was such a narrow space Rotem had to squeeze to get in, which is part of what saved him. Debbie draped herself on top of Rotem. Moments later, the attackers forced the door open. An explosion went off in the room—a hand grenade— filling the air with smoke. Rotem heard his dad yell, "I lost my arm."

Then many attackers were inside, and everything was chaos.

"They got in and started shooting everywhere," Rotem told me.

Rotem felt an odd taste in his mouth, and then a hot sensation in his stomach. He lay as still as he could. He's not sure how long the shooting continued, but then it stopped and Rotem heard the attackers laughing as they left the room.

His mother, still above him, wasn't moving. He could tell she was no longer alive. He felt that he had no choice but to remain lying there quietly beneath her.

"I laid under my mom's body for 45 minutes," said Rotem. "My bed is tall and my mom was above me, so they didn't see me."

At 8:01—17 minutes after Debbie sent her last text—Rotem took out his own phone with his mother's body still on top of him and messaged the family group.

"Mom and dad r dead sorry," he texted. "Call help."

By that, he told me, he meant he was sorry they had to hear about it that way.

A minute later, Aron's daughter Gabriella—Rotem's cousin— texted, "How"

At this point, his sister Shir texted the chat for the first time, "What, its not funny."

That was the state of disbelief.

"Please," was all Rotem could respond.

Then Shir texted: "be quiet. Sit quiet. It will be OK rotem."

At 8:04, Rotem texted simply, "Blood."

A moment later, his Uncle Abie asked, "Rotem where are you"

Rotem responded, "Bed under"

"Are you under the bed, Rotem?" asked his sister Shir.

"No next"

"Where are Mom and Dad," Shir asked.

"Dead"

Another relative on the Troen chat asked at 8:07: "Rotem we love you. Stay strong and safe."

"Thanks."

"Is anyone home with you?" Shir asked at 8:08.

Rotem seemed to think she meant the attackers. "I got shot," he texted. "No. They are gone. It hurts."

"What. Where," asked Shir.

"Stomach," typed Rotem.

"Put pressure on the wound," his sister told him.

His next text must have been terrifying to the family.

"Someone got in," Rotem messaged. "Fuck." He meant the militants had come back.

At 8:10, someone on the chat asked if he could speak on the phone—or will it make noise?

"Don't," someone texted.

Whoever came back set fire to something in the house, prompting Rotem to send a string of texts.

"Please"

Then these successive messages:

"Too much smoke cant breathe."

"Help"

"No. Don't call me"

"They will hear"

"Hard to see"

Shir texted the family that she and her sister were keeping quiet for safety in their own flats. The threat was everywhere.

At 8:13, Rotem texted: "Help. Blood. It hurts."

"You'll be okay, Rotem," Shir wrote back. "I know."

At 8:14, Rotem answered: "I Love u all just in case."

He added: "Moms body is on me. I can't move."

"Be strong," a family member texted. "You will get through this. Your parents spirit is with you."

They told him help was on the way, but that proved wishful thinking. It would be over 10 hours.

Rotem of course didn't know it would take that long, but felt that between the wound and the attackers, he might not last even minutes.

"No time," Rotem texted at 8:18. "Help"

The family texted among themselves about getting security forces there.

At 8:19, Rotem messaged: "I'm going to pass out. No air. Bombs. Help."

His Uncle Abie wrote: "Help is on the way." Which they believed because of their faith in the Israeli army, but it wasn't true.

"Gun shot," texted Rotem. "Don't call" Then simply: "Pls"

Two minutes later at 8:22 he added: "Fuzzy sight. I cant see"

Shani, his cousin, is a social worker. "What do you see," she texted. "What is around you."

"Bed. I'm stuck." That text came at 8:23.

Rotem had by now been lying under his mom's body for almost a half hour.

Shani texted, "Can you see anything around you."

"Blood."

At this point, Shir and Shakked, hiding in their own apartments, went silent on the chat, and would remain so for eight hours as they ignored knocks on their doors. At times, they heard screaming and explosions. At various points, the Hamas killers shined flashlights through their windows.

"They were just lucky," my friend Michael told me when I talked to him. "Who knows?"

Smoke was continuing to fill the room where Rotem lay. It got even harder for him to breathe.

At last, he felt he had no choice but to get from under his mother's body. Almost 45 minutes after he first hid under her, he crawled free, stood, and saw what happened. His mother had died of wounds from both bullets and shards from the explosions. He's sure it was both.

"She one hundred percent got shrapnel," Rotem told me.

His father was dead too. He was missing an arm and had other shrapnel wounds. Rotem believes his father bled to death.

The hot sensation in his abdomen remained, so Rotem took off his shirt. That's when he saw a bullet hole. The bullet had also grazed his arm after going through the bed.

He saw pieces of flesh on the wall, and realized the strange taste in his mouth earlier was likely from bits of his father's body after the hand grenade exploded.

I paused to ask if he was comfortable with me putting that detail in the account I was writing.

"Yes."

Carefully, he stepped out of his room to see where the smoke was coming from. It turned out they had lit a living room couch on fire.

"To get anyone out of the house so they can shoot them," Rotem told me.

At 8:33, he texted his family, "I'm not in the room anymore."

He could still hear the attackers nearby and worried they'd come back. Rotem tried to cover his mouth so he wouldn't cough from the smoke and draw attention.

He felt he should hide somewhere safer. Their home had an attached laundry room built to be entered only through an outside door, so he left the house and quickly went into the room. He noticed his ankle was bleeding too, likely from hand grenade shrapnel. He found a cloth and tied it around the ankle.

Rotem spent the next hours hiding in the laundry room. At times he covered himself with bedding to remain unseen. Now and then, he stood to try to see what was happening. At one point, as he looked out the room's window, an RPG shell whizzed by, and he heard an explosion. The shooting continued, too.

After a while, the smoke from the house seemed to have lessened, so he snuck back in.

"I saw my dad's body," said Rotem. "And I saw a pool of blood."

The whole house was black from soot. Rotem noticed cobwebs that had turned black, too.

At 10:53, in a whisper, he recorded a WhatsApp voice message to his family group saying, "I'm back home. There isn't really any smoke. But now I can actually say, Mom and Dad aren't alive." On the recording, he started to cry. "I'm so sorry."

Others sent him love.

"I am sad," Rotem messaged by voice at 10:55, "but at least I'm alive. And I can keep...remembering them."

Then the sound of yelling in Arabic got closer, so he felt he should hide again. This time, he went into his parents' room and hid between that bed and wall. It was just in time. A moment later, he heard the men enter the house.

"You could hear every single step," Rotem told me. "I knew where they were. They were opening drawers and closets and taking things."

Then they came into the very bedroom where he was hiding.

"I heard someone right by me," Rotem told me. "But they left, luckily."

He decided to stay hiding there in the house. Hours went by. Periodically, he would text with his family.

As time passed, he stayed on the Troen WhatsApp group. Several doctors on the chat, including Rotem's aunt and a family friend, had him take selfies of his abdominal wound, advising on how to stop the bleeding. Another person on the chat was a niece of my high school friend Michael, Bar Yuval-Shani, a trauma psychotherapist.

"That's a big industry in Israel," Michael told me. "She goes to where the rockets are and gives aid to people who are, I don't know what the word is, falling apart."

Yuval-Shani was one of many on the chat who worked to get Rotem through. When he grew hopeless and said he was unable to do anything to help himself, she told him that waiting is a form of action and bravery.

"They literally kept him alive," Michael told me. "Several times he said, 'I can't anymore. I have to let it go.' And they said, 'No, you're a hero.'"

It went like that for 10 hours. Even when the Israeli army arrived, there was a long firefight.

Kibbutz Holit, only a mile from Gaza, was mostly destroyed during the Hamas attack.

"There were dozens of them," Michael said of the terrorists still in the kibbutz. "They had to go from house to house."

Rotem was hiding under some covers when he heard men

talking in Hebrew. He had been warned militants sometimes use Hebrew as a ruse, so he didn't move. Then the men talking in Hebrew touched the cover he was under. Realizing someone was there, they told him not to move.

"I said, 'Please don't kill me,'" Rotem recalled. "I'm wounded."

He saw they were indeed IDF, and he had been rescued.

As the soldiers escorted him outside, Rotem told them that both his parents were murdered. He looked around the kibbutz and was stunned. Almost all the buildings had been destroyed or damaged. Many houses, including that of his immediate neighbor, had been burned down. There were bodies everywhere. One of the bodies he saw had its head split open and brain matter on the ground.

An army medic checked Rotem's abdomen, but many others were gravely wounded and needed attention, so he was taken to neighbors who helped treat him. By then, the hole in his stomach had stopped bleeding. Rotem later learned adrenaline can do that, even though the bullet remained inside him.

Because there were still terrorists in the area, the soldiers transferred Rotem to various armored vehicles to get him out of danger, and finally to an ambulance. During his rescue, he continued to see more bodies of neighbors, as well as militants. Cars had been burnt or blown up. There was a tank on fire. Clearly, it had been a brutal fight.

The ambulance took him to Soroka Medical Center in the biggest nearby city, Be'er Sheva, where his grandfather Ilan teaches at Ben Gurion University. The hospital staff was overwhelmed with hundreds of people waiting to be treated.

"I saw people holding their limbs together so they wouldn't fall apart," said Rotem. "It took me over an hour to get into the emergency surgery room."

Right before the surgery, around 8:30 p.m., his sister Shir reached him by phone call. It was the first he'd talked to her the whole day. The sound of her voice made Rotem break down and weep.

Surgeons removed the bullet, and Rotem decided to keep it as a memory of the need to survive, and what his parents sacrificed for him.

I asked Aron if he had any photos of his nephew Rotem's destroyed home in Kibbutz Holit. He sent me this closeup of a pin amidst soot and shattered glass, reflecting the family's belief in coexistence, ironically shared by all the targeted Jewish communities near Gaza.

Rotem's family tried to protect him from hearing all that had happened on Oct. 7, but he soon called friends, who told him about the hostages, and that over 1,000 Israelis had been killed. The news stunned him.

"I hadn't understood how big it all was," he told me.

I asked how he was doing now compared to right after the attack.

"Physically better," he said. "Mentally worse."

Why worse?

"Because I don't give myself the right treatment I need," Rotem said. "I'm not as active in that as I should be."

How does it show?

"I don't watch TV anymore," said Rotem. "I don't play video games. I usually stay in my room in the dark, staring at the ceiling." He no longer feels safe in his home.

I asked what he thinks about at such times.

"I don't know," said Rotem. "Usually I just imagine a world where I'm happier. Where it didn't happen. Or I'll just remember that day."

He has gone to many kinds of therapists but hasn't overly connected with them.

"There aren't really any experts in these kinds of situations," said Rotem. "Nobody really knows how to deal with it."

I asked what he means by "it"?

"The situation of being that close to death. Seeing your parents murdered in front of you. Somebody being exposed to cruelty and evil. Not feeling safe anymore."

Was there a reason he agreed to talk about it with me?

"It's important for people to understand."

And also, he added, because many now say it didn't happen.

Why does he think they would deny it?

"People want to justify what happened," he said. "And say it's freedom fighters or whatever. That's just blind." Denial, he said, also lets them keep hating "certain groups." Those were his words, but he clearly meant Jews.

Rotem struck me as more mature than his age of 16, including physically. He is tall and in good shape with a three-or-four-day beard growth.

Was there anything he'd want to tell others going through trauma?

"No, nobody goes through it the same way. Even if they went through the same thing, they see it differently. What's helpful to me might not help somebody else."

Has he spoken with others who endured similar?

"No," Rotem said, "usually when terrorists get in your house, you won't survive. When you're shot you won't survive. There's a very small chance someone would survive something like this."

I told him it seemed a good sign, perhaps of strength, that he was able to talk about it.

I think he nodded slightly to that, but I'm not sure.

Finally, I asked if I could see the wound. He pulled up his shirt to show it. Three months later, there was still a clear mark.

Then he agreed to stand for some photos, with his Uncle Aron behind him.

By now, Aron's daughter Gabriella—Rotem's cousin—had come downstairs. She was working on a school project. She's 17 and one of her career thoughts is journalism. We talked about that for a few minutes, and dinner was being made, and you realized this was what many Israeli families are like, dealing with trauma, but life having to go on.

It was after 10 p.m. when Aron dropped me at my hotel in Jerusalem. He said it will be a long time before Rotem works through this, and of course, in many ways he never will. Who could?

As I settled in my room, I thought back to first hearing about Rotem in the phone call with my high school friend Michael. That interview went over an hour. As it got close to finishing, Michael began speaking in the background to his wife. That brings up why I am not using his last name. His wife was asking him to leave it out.

Michael told me her mother was the only member of her family to survive the Holocaust. The mother's siblings and other family were exterminated in Auschwitz and Buchenwald.

The murder of her niece had stirred that up, convincing her that the same kind of Jew hatred that led to the death camps is back again. Some of the pro-Palestinian rallies that celebrated the Hamas murders have particularly frightened her, as have videos of protesters shouting for death to Zionists. There in Chicago, where Michael and his wife were staying with their son, they saw police posted with automatic weapons at nearby temples.

I had told Michael that it would be better for the story to use his full name, and that's what his wife was reacting to in the background—he had asked her if she was comfortable with it.

Now he told me she wasn't.

I said I understood, but would it be all right for him to ask her one more time? Perhaps tell her that a full name would add weight to the message here about the dangers of antisemitism?

As he asked his wife again, I heard her start to cry in a panicky tone. It was a wrenching sound. I heard her say the word "please" several times, basically choking it out.

That's when I told Michael that of course, I would leave his last name out.

"I've been sleeping the last few nights with a loaded gun next to my bed," he said, "because she is deathly afraid people will come into our house and kill us."

He added that he has some of the same concerns. He often dresses in a way that's visibly Jewish, for example wearing an Orthodox black hat.

"I always watch for oncoming traffic," Michael said. "Are they going to swerve and hit me, or run me over, or put a gun out of the window and shoot at me?"

I told him it's terrible to have to worry about such things.

"That's the world we live in," Michael said.

There on the phone, he paused to again assure his wife that their last name would not be used.

But she continued sobbing.

I am sure for many reasons.

Inside Gaza, I made my way down an excavated dirt ramp to a tunnel where Hamas militants ran out to attack Israel. Major Nir, age 66, posted nearby, told me, "It's not near the border, it's on the border." (Photo by Robby Berman)

EIGHTEEN

INSIDE THE BATTLEFIELD

T he rain came down hard the morning I was due to go into
Gaza, moving in off the Mediterranean as it usually does, and
perhaps it was just as well. They say it's often too cold or hot or wet
in a war, so maybe this was the way to see it.

But by the time we dozen journalists gather at 10 a.m. at an
IDF deployment spot just outside the strip, the storm is over, the
sky leaden, the air cool enough that you are glad for the extra layer
of the required bulletproof vests.

It is the first time the IDF has taken reporters inside in three or
so weeks. Among our stops, we are told, will be a tunnel destroyed

the night before. It ran from the nearby Khan Yunis refugee camp, where fighting is now heavy, under the no-man's land buffer along the border fence, ending so close it took less than a minute for scores of Hamas to charge into Israel on that terrible day. That's the only thing the tunnel was for.

Our assigned overseer is Lt. Col. Anshi, first names only. He's a 46-year-old tech guy who, like countless Israelis, has been called to war.

Among those here for the embed are correspondents with CBS and Fox News, as well as counterparts from other countries. Anshi courteously asks us to turn off our phone locations—no one wants a surprise.

We squeeze into a pair of side-bench Humvees, then start speeding just outside the border fence to our left, splashing through puddles and sandy mud. On our right are bountiful banana trees belonging to a nearby kibbutz where dozens were slaughtered, and each time soldiers go by it, they are reminded of why they are here.

For the first time in three weeks, the IDF took selected members of the press into Gaza. The Humvee ride was a tight squeeze. (Photo by Mark Patinkin)

Every few seconds, military vehicles fly past us going the other way, heading back to base. Israeli combat soldiers don't drive slowly. Our Humvee has a canvas top, open sides and a front-mounted belt-fed machine gun. The vehicle bounces over ruts, wind whipping loudly around us.

Suddenly, we turn left through a gap in the fence.

Lt. Col. Anshi would soon tell us it's one of the breaks blown apart by Hamas on their way to invade Israel. You can't help but note the irony of the IDF using it to attack back.

The Gaza side is open terrain, weedy and treeless, left fallow as a buffer. Soon, we pull up to a spot with big piles of tan dirt, excavated to reveal the tunnel.

"Welcome to Gaza," says Anshi as we step out of the Humvee.

So far, because there are no buildings, I don't see the familiar images of dystopia. But Anshi says we'll get there soon.

At that, there's an enormous boom—a helicopter-fired missile, he says. One of the front lines, explains Anshi, is less than a mile away in dense Khan Yunis. An hour from now, I would hear a more unsettling sound of war. I'll get to that in a moment.

A steep dirt ramp has been bulldozed down to the tunnel's mouth 20 feet below. It makes you realize how Hamas kept them secret. They built them deep, using narrow, vertical shafts for access. But the shaft here has been plowed away and an open pit now surrounds the tunnel two stories beneath us.

"We were surprised by the scope of it," says Anshi. It runs all the way to Khan Yunis, he adds, then connects to the Gaza "subway." We're now looking at the end of it, where the attackers came out.

Two at a time, we walk and slide down the excavated ramp, our boots sinking ankle-deep into the loose earth. IDF troops posted along it put out hands to keep us from falling. When I get to the bottom, a burly soldier named Major Nir is next to the opening.

"It's so close to the border," I say.

As I crawled to the opening of a Hamas tunnel to look inside, I was struck by the engineering, and couldn't help but imagine how much good could have been built in Gaza with such resources. (Photo by Robby Berman)

Major Nir shakes his head. "It's not near the border," he says, "it's on the border."

Nir's five-day beard growth is white. It turns out he's 66 and a businessman but volunteered to do his part. His son is now at Khan Yunis, also in the fight. It worries Nir as a dad, but this is where both feel they need to be.

I slide past Nir down the last 8 feet to look directly inside. The tunnel's top is reinforced with curved concrete, and I find myself thinking, here it is—one of the spots where it began, a war that has upended the world.

For a few minutes, I lie there on my side in the dirt, sand in my boots, looking down it. A nearby soldier aims a gun-mounted beam to light up the interior for me. It's shadowy and creepy in there, more so because you know what it was used for. We're not able to go in because a demolition crew blew up the middle of it last night. Although it has been said before, when you actually see such a tunnel—the engineering, the shaped concrete, the massive effort—you're stunned at how much good could have been built in Gaza with such resources. You also realize how long Hamas had been planning for war. We are told this tunnel took a year or more to construct.

As other pairs of journalists slide down, I head up to ground level and chat with Anshi. I've learned by now that almost everyone in Israel has an Oct. 7 story. In Anshi's case, he was awakened by missiles that morning, and the next day was deployed with the job of collecting civilian bodies.

Anshi has two kids, 19 and 15. He spent a few of his younger years in Boston when his physician dad worked at the Dana Farber cancer hospital.

That's when I hear the sound that's more unsettling than explosions, though not as loud. It's automatic weapons fire, closer than I expected. It goes nonstop for many minutes and makes you picture what that kind of fighting must be like.

"It's a skirmish," says Anshi. "There's no big armor-versus-armor. It's terrorists coming out of a hole and shooting."

"How close?" I ask.

"Twenty to 30 meters," he says. "Or less. Everything is close."

Indeed, most Israeli soldiers carry rifles with shortened stocks so they can swing them around corners without being overly exposed. That is how urban war is being fought in 2024.

Early on, Anshi says too many Israelis were killed because of mistakes. When a Gaza civilian called for help, or a Hamas soldier darted away, IDF troops would run toward them. But it was usually a trap.

"We paid a heavy price for that," Anshi said. "There was a lot of learning."

And it's still a dilemma, with unarmed "civilians" walking innocently with others, then running into a house where they've stashed weapons.

We spend a half hour around the tunnel—or maybe it's an hour; it's easy to lose track. At one point, I approach a soldier who gives his name as Zori. He is 33 and on Oct. 7, was in Kfar Azza, a targeted kibbutz with 60 murdered and 20 taken. Zori hid in his basement for a dozen hours with his wife and two kids, ages 2 and 18 months. He says God saved them, adding he's here so it won't happen again.

Finally, we squeeze back into the Humvees and start speeding toward our next stop—an elementary school Hamas used as a base.

"Every school," says Anshi. "Every mosque. Every health facility."

During one stretch, our Humvee passed a mile-long destroyed neighborhood, a post-apocalyptic sight. (Photo by Mark Patinkin)

As we head that way, the terrain changes and we reporters fall silent. We've entered dystopia, a treeless suburb where big stone homes with a half-acre around each unfold in a mile-long neighborhood. You can tell that those who lived here had some wealth, and you wonder again why Hamas provoked a war sacrificing all this. It's post-apocalyptic, many of the villas in this once-upscale area turned to rubble, similar to a tornado scene except worse because the earth is disrupted, too.

You assume this area is safe, but nowhere in Gaza is, so the Humvee drivers keep flooring it, bucking through dips with little braking. At last, we pull up to a large, battle-scarred elementary school, three stories high with two wings. It's now an IDF staging area with parked tanks and vehicles coming and going.

We step out and gather around Anshi, who says they recently took the school from militants in a nighttime battle. Then they secured it, or thought they did. The next morning, four Hamas came out of a missed basement tunnel shaft and began firing. Two of Anshi's men were killed in seconds. So were three of the Hamas militants, the fourth escaping back down. Moments after that battle, as Anshi walked by a door of the school, a sniper bullet went through the flesh of his left arm. That, he says, is the kind of war it is—the enemy comes out of both the ground and nowhere.

It's the reason most houses we just drove past were destroyed by the IDF. That stays with me as a terrible sight, a neighborhood demolished. But Israeli soldiers ask, what do you do when militants hide in it with RPGs and anti-tank missiles waiting to kill you?

I approach another soldier who is trying to light a cigarette, needing three tries because of the wind before he gets it. He gives his name as Bar, 26, and says he was on vacation in Thailand when Oct. 7 happened. He left immediately and was back on Oct. 8, assigned to help tow burnt cars at the Nova music site to a gathering point. Later, some were found to have human remains inside, at first overlooked because the interiors were melted. It would take a while to do such forensic work. Bar also saw bodies of Hamas militants still on the ground. He lost a dozen friends and colleagues the day of the attack.

We stopped at a Gaza elementary school the IDF took back from Hamas, which stored weapons there. "Every school," said Lt. Col. Anshi, our guide. "Every mosque. Every health facility." (Photo by Mark Patinkin)

Bar's grandparents used to tell him about Jews being murdered in pogroms in Russia, which seemed far in the past. But now it had happened again, right here, the same kind of hate, and that, he said, is why he fights, so Israel can be safe.

At that, there is a blast so loud that things around us shake, a bit of dust rising from the earth. A soldier says it was a bomb from an Israeli plane. We are close enough that 20 seconds later smoke wafts across us with a fireworks smell.

Beyond the school, the landscape looks like a cliche war movie scene after a battle. It's a tableau of destruction, the ground scarred by vehicle tracks and broken buildings with plumes of dark smoke in the distance.

I find myself looking at a nearby Israeli tank and it brings back a memory from the early 1990s.

I was in Israel with a group led by an older tour guide who had arranged to take us to an Israeli Army base. It was in an unpopulated area surrounded by hills. I remember the guide's name as Gadi. He was mid-60s and a Holocaust survivor, but upbeat and energetic. He had thick gray hair and was around 5-foot-6. At one point, some soldiers rolled out a tank to do a demonstration for our group. They had us step back as the gunner swiveled the turret toward a hillside. A minute later, the tank fired a shell that exploded in fire against the steep ground 100 yards away. Or maybe it was 50.

At the sight of it, Gadi made an excited jump, fists clenched in pride as he half-shouted, "We are so *strong*." And then he said it again. He had once been helpless in a death camp, and now he had tanks. I'll always remember that as a glimpse of the Israeli psyche.

We aren't allowed to go into the school itself, but Anshi gives us time to do interviews, standups and photos. Every soldier I approach is open to chatting, and has the same take—after Oct. 7, there's no question they need to be fighting this war. They are reservists in the army's 55th Infantry Brigade. Its nickname is "Tip of the Spear" since they fight at the front lines. The brigade has 3,000 soldiers, and so far, Anshi says they've lost 12—a high casualty rate for Israel. During their months here, the 55th has found and destroyed 70 shafts, a reminder of how the tunnels work. It's not just one entry and exit. Most have scores of shafts allowing militants to pop up and ambush at will.

"Ninety percent are booby-trapped," Anshi says, "and they try to lure us in."

Nearby, explosions seem to go off every few minutes—sometimes seconds. IDF vehicles continue to come and go from the courtyard. By the school walls, there are tangles of razor wire beneath cartoon murals of kids at play. Next to one of the murals, there is a blasted hole in the building the size of a garage door. Blue and white Israeli flags are draped over a few upper floor balconies.

The walls around the flags have dozens of bullet marks. Beyond the building, in an open field, there are long rows of perimeter razor wire to keep out infiltrators.

One of the IDF soldiers in Gaza told me his grandparents used to talk about Jews being murdered in pogroms in Russia around 1900, which seemed far in the past to him—until Oct. 7. That, he told me, is why he fights, so Israel can be safe. (Photo by Mark Patinkin)

None of the soldiers around us carry a light load. Their vests, fortified with bullet-proof plates, have a dozen or so chest-pockets bulging with ammunition, radios and other gear. Each man has an automatic rifle and a sidearm. All wear leather gloves, helmets, propped-up goggles and neck gaiters that could be pulled over the mouth and nose to protect against sand. Their boots are caked with mud, most with pants cuffs tucked in. Though the sun is now emerging, there are puddles everywhere. Muddy Humvee tracks disappear in and out of them.

At last, Anshi says it's time to go—embed trips like this are tightly scripted. Soon, our Humvees are speeding back across the same dystopian landscape we had come through on the way here. For every house left standing, there are three or more turned to debris. The sight is so mesmerizing I simply stare before remembering to take video for my job. The Humvee is moving fast as I aim my phone camera, but the video goes for minutes—that's how much destruction there is.

I've rewatched that video often, and each time, it makes you wonder how Gaza can ever be whole again. And whether Israel needed to do this much damage. But you wonder more why Hamas doesn't free the hostages and save what's left of their homeland.

Our two Humvees turn back through the hole in the border fence, leaving Gaza behind, and finally, we arrive at our original staging area. They tell us the information from the trip is embargoed for 24 hours because it could put troops in jeopardy.

The clouds have now receded, and as my guide Robby and I begin the drive home to Jerusalem, I see a contrast that to me is a symbol of Israel.

It's a beautiful citrus grove that goes on and on, the sun reflecting off thousands of Jaffa oranges.

So much promise.

But so close to the border.

And the sounds of war that follow us as we drive.

It was difficult connecting with Palestinian folks enduring the war inside Gaza, but late one night, Hisham Mhanna answered his phone and told me of his life there. His Palestinian-Filipino wife had evacuated and later given birth to a son Hisham had yet to meet. But as a Red Cross worker, Hisham felt he is needed in Gaza. (Photo courtesy of Hisham Mhanna)

NINETEEN

VOICES FROM GAZA

And now in my hotel in Jerusalem, seeking a glimpse into Gaza from the other side, I keep dialing numbers of people within it. I had collected contact information for 30 or so prospects. I try half a dozen doctors, but none answer. Clearly, both they and Gaza's cell systems are overwhelmed.

I had gotten names of business people too, but no luck. I try on and off for days.

And then, one night, as I try again, I get an answer.

It's Dr. Abdullatif Alhaj, head of Gaza's European Hospital in Khan Yunis.

Soon, I learn why I had gotten through.

I'd reached him not in Gaza, but Istanbul, where he'd taken his two war-wounded grandchildren. He told me they are among the only ones in his wider family who survived an airstrike on his home. He is all they have now, so he brought them to safety.

Dr. Alhaj is 59. At first, we had a bit of trouble with the connection, but he gave me a half-hour so I could understand what he and Gaza have been through.

As head of one of Gaza's bigger hospitals, he saw the war's impact immediately.

"There was quickly an accumulation of injured," Alhaj says. "Four or five times the capacity of each hospital."

So many critical patients were backed up that doctors had to first treat the worst cases to save lives, knowing the ones waiting would lose limbs.

More than 50 of Alhaj's extended family, many of them children, had been displaced from their homes by the bombardment. They started sheltering in his house, declared by the Israelis to be in a safe area. In late November, Dr. Alhaj was working overnight when he was given terrible news. His house had been hit in an Israeli strike. It was 4 a.m., so almost all were home and sleeping.

When Dr. Alhaj rushed over, he found most in the house had been crushed by the rubble. Dr. Alhaj's voice was more quiet than angry as he described it, like someone left drained from trauma.

"A massacre actually," he says. "My son and his wife and child. My daughter and her husband and their child also. My sister, my little son, 17 years old; all those have been killed." And more.

When I later searched online for the incident, I saw mention of the loss of his daughter on the World Health Organization's website.

Her name was Dima Alhaj. She was 29 and since 2019, had been a patient administrator with WHO's Limb Reconstruction Centre in Gaza City in the north of the strip. She once posted on social media that she loved her work because, in her words, "It contributes to giving people hope and a new lease on life."

Dima had evacuated four times because of the war, finally seeking shelter in her parents' home in southern Gaza.

The WHO report confirmed Dr. Alhaj's count—around 50 family and friends were killed in the strike, including Dima's husband Mohammed and their 6-month-old son, Aboud.

Dima had received an Earth Sciences degree at the Islamic University of Gaza as well as a master's at Glasgow University in Scotland as part of a European Union student exchange program.

Dr. Rik Peeperkorn is WHO's Gaza rep, a prominent figure there, and knew Dima well.

"She was a wonderful person with a radiant smile, cheerful, positive, respectful," he said in a WHO post about her loss.

Now, Dr. Alhaj tells me by phone that among the few survivors of the strike were his wife Aya, one of their daughters, and the two grandchildren with him now in Istanbul.

"One of them, 8 years old, is suffering from the fracture of the hip," Dr. Alhaj says. That's his grandson.

His granddaughter survived too, despite being impossibly young.

"Her age was two weeks when she got the trauma," says Dr. Alhaj. "You can imagine how little she is. She had a severe head injury and brain hemorrhage."

For a few seconds, Dr. Alhaj is silent on the phone, composing himself.

"It's why we are here now," he finally says, "for further management."

Dr. Alhaj grew up in Gaza's Nuseirat refugee camp, later doing medical training in both Jerusalem and Japan. For years, he's been head of Gaza's European Hospital, but he feels at the moment his job as a grandfather is most important.

I ask if he liked Gaza before the war.

"Yes, of course," says Dr. Alhaj. "It's my home. All my family is there. My extended family. It's my people. My homeland. And I had a mission we had to do."

Does he plan to go back?

"I don't know. Gaza is not Gaza now. We don't have a house; it was destroyed. The majority of my family was killed. I don't know."

He tells me he will weigh that later; his focus now is his two orphaned grandchildren.

Dr. Abdullatif Alhaj had long been head of Gaza's European Hospital, but I reached him by phone in Turkey, where he was taking care of his two grandchildren, wounded when an Israeli bomb hit his family home, killing dozens of his loved ones.

"They are without their father, without their mother," he says. "Now I choose to be their father and their mother."

It is close to 10 p.m. as we talk, Jerusalem and Istanbul being in the same time zone, and I feel I shouldn't hold him longer.

"You sound like a good man," I say in bidding him goodbye.

Dr. Alhaj responds with one word.

"Inshalla."

Over the next evenings, I continue making calls and at last manage to connect live with someone inside Gaza. He is a likely candidate to be reached since his job is to be available. His name is Hisham Mhanna, a young communications guy for the International Committee of the Red Cross since 2019. Before that, he had similar jobs in Gaza with both Catholic Relief Services and Save the Children. In 2012, he spent a year studying at New York University. He speaks Hebrew as well as Arabic and English.

But I am more interested in him personally.

Hisham is 34 and grew up in Gaza City, the son of a contractor.

I ask his mom's job.

"A terrific mother."

Hisham has two children, one of whom he hadn't met yet when we spoke. His wife is half Palestinian and half Filipino, so was eligible to be evacuated in November, when she was close to giving birth. Their new son, Jude, is just 2 months old, and Hisham has seen him only in photos and video calls. His other son, Ryan, is 2 and a half.

Why did Hisham choose to stay?

"I still have the rest of my family here," he says. "My parents, my brothers, my sisters, my nephews and nieces."

And he believes in his work.

Since he's a Red Cross spokesperson, it's important for Hisham to be neutral. So, on this late January night in 2024, he simply shares with me what he has seen and been through.

He used to live in one of Gaza's nicer neighborhoods, in southwest Tel al-Hawa, near the Mediterranean. But most of that area has been destroyed.

"The café where we hang out," says Hisham, "and our favorite restaurant. The place where I studied in college." All gone now.

Like most people in Gaza, Hisham has lost family, friends and colleagues. One of those colleagues, a 40ish Red Cross radio operator named Abdo, hasn't been buried yet. The building that collapsed on him after an airstrike is unstable, and with so many similar collapses, there isn't enough equipment to extract the bodies.

I ask if he and Abdo were close.

"He was the nicest guy you could have your morning coffee with," says Hisham.

Abdo's wife and 8-year-old son survived and now, like so many, are living as displaced people in Gaza's south. Before the war, said Hisham, that area was already crowded with 300,000—today there are 1.5 million.

Hisham is now based near there, too, in Rafah, where he has worked for five years. When he can, he goes with Red Cross teams to deliver medicine to hospitals, as well as items like blankets to the displaced.

I feel I have to ask him about an ICRC controversy. Hostage families in Israel are angry that the Red Cross hasn't visited the kidnapped—one of their official missions. I checked Hisham's feed on X, where he periodically reports needs in the field, and in some cases, his posts draw comments along the lines of, "Why aren't you visiting the hostages?"

It remains a goal, Hisham tells me, but he explains it this way: "All parties have to guarantee access and security." And that hasn't happened.

"We cannot force ourselves," he tells me.

Of course, that is shorthand for Hamas refuses.

But it goes both ways. In response, Israel has barred the Red Cross from visiting the thousands of Palestinians imprisoned since Oct. 7 until Hamas allows access to hostages.

I ask Hisham how people are getting by in the crowded south.

"They can't put food on the table," he says. "There's not even a table. They live in tents and the streets."

Some families, he says, have had to evacuate a half-dozen times, and they may face it again. He also sees unsettling signs of mental-health problems.

"I have witnessed women crying by the bodies of their husbands, or parents, or children," Hisham says, "and the next week they would be sitting there silently. It expresses trauma."

As I was working on this book in the months after returning from the Middle East, I wondered how Hisham Mhanna was doing so searched his name. A part of me worried I might find tragic news about him. Or perhaps hopeful news that he had finally left to join his family and see his new son for the first time.

It turned out he was still there, performing his work. I saw him recently quoted in a story in the Arab News about hospitals in Gaza barely able to function.

"There are still casualties who are scheduled for operations that cannot be performed because there are no supplies, no anesthetic drugs, no generators," Hisham said. "It's a mess. It's a catastrophe."

I also checked Hisham's feed on X.

"In 16 yrs," Hisham posted April 3, "people in Gaza managed to survive a prolonged blockade, 6 devastating conflicts, cyclic escalations & staggering levels of poverty & unemployment. Their ability to resurrect is impossible this time. They've lost everything. Entire generations lost the power of hope."

Having seen a needy but intact Gaza in 1991 myself, and a Gaza half-destroyed in 2024, that resonated with me.

It's a testament to Hisham that he is still there. He could leave, join his family, see his youngest for the first time—but as I write this in early July, he remains committed to staying. His most recent X post was from July 2, saying, "Thousands of children, elderly, sick & injured spent last night on the streets with no shelter in Khan Younis. This must not become their normal life."

When I asked Hisham Mhanna why he remained in Gaza after his wife and kids had evacuated, he told me it's where he's needed, and the people are grateful every time he heads out to help, as he prepares to do here in the southern part of the strip.

In mid-July, I decided to try Hisham by text one last time, and was surprised to reach him. I asked if he had finally met his new son Jude.

"Not yet," Hisham texted back. "He has turned 9 months on July 10th. He started eating, crawling and he has his dolphin teeth now." Hisham added a smile emoji.

Then he sent a voice message saying that despite the war—really because of it—his work, though heartbreaking, remains hugely meaningful. He fields dozens of calls a day from folks desperate for aid or information about loved ones.

"I'm trying to give anyone the help I can give," he said. He added that all are incredibly thankful—as Hisham is thankful to be doing humanitarian work in a place where the need is so great.

As we finish our phone conversation in January, I ask Hisham if he plans to remain in Gaza once the war ends.

"I love my home here," Hisham tells me, "but there's no home left."

So much of Gaza, he says, is quite literally rubble. Would his kids and family have schools? Electricity and water infrastructure? Not for a long time.

Then I ask Hisham whom he blames.

"War is ugly for everyone on both sides of the border line," he says. "For all families."

I thank him for giving a powerful glimpse from inside.

"I've seen a lot, my friend," he says.

I have one more question: Has this changed him?

"Hello?" Hisham says. "Mark?"

I ask again, but we could no longer hear each other. And then, in a telling moment, the connection goes dead, and both he, and Gaza, are out of reach.

I spent a half hour with Zak Mishriki, owner of the notable Zak's Antiquities Shop in the Old City. When I asked his background, Zak told me he doesn't say Israeli or Palestinian: "I say Jerusalemite. To avoid myself from the politics." (Photo by Mark Patinkin)

TWENTY

JERUSALEM, AGAIN

One last time before I leave Israel, I am drawn to the Old City, to hear its voices during this difficult time.

Voices like Ahmed's.

He owns one of the first stores you walk past inside the Jaffa Gate, his wares a display of coexistence. He sells crosses for Christians, Hamsa hands for Muslims and Stars of David for Jews.

Ahmed's is among the few shops in the Old City still open after what war has done to tourism here.

"May I make you tea?" he says as I pause to look.

It gets me smiling at his merchant skills. One usually isn't offered tea at The Gap.

"Thank you," I say, "but no need."

"Don't break my heart," says Ahmed, who is 37. "May I call you brother?"

I notice yarmulkes and keffiyehs side by side on his shelves, just as I saw Judaica in a West Bank shop near the Church of the Nativity, and it makes you realize how commerce bridges the divide.

I ask how business is.

"Thank God," Ahmed responds, then adds: "This is what we always say—thank God for good things, and not good things. Thank God."

"How," I ask, "has it been going since the war?"

"I don't like politics." Ahmed says. "I believe in people. Like you. I believe a miracle is coming."

Where is he from?

He tells me he has a Jordanian green card and an Israeli ID.

"It's complicated here, my brother."

I make a few purchases, raising Ahmed's hopes for more. Do I have a wife or girlfriend? Daughters or sisters? Because look here—so beautiful what he has for them.

Sold—one more item, which gets him offering tea again, but it's time to move on.

I continue down narrow David Street, which paradoxically goes through the Arab Quarter, a tunnel-like alleyway as moody as any ancient path in this world. Usually, it's a bustling souk for Christian pilgrims, prayerful Jews and devout Muslims. Not these days.

Soon, I turn left down the similar Christian Quarter Road, a reminder of how tightly woven the faiths are here. I stop to chat with another Arab proprietor, Awni, 57, asking him about the war.

Business, he says, has been hard.

"We are tired from the politics we have," he tells me. His Israeli and Palestinian friends want to live in peace. Others I speak with say the same.

Just inside the Old City, I found Ahmed, who owns a store selling crosses for Christians, Hamsa hands for Muslims and Stars of David for Jews. "I don't like politics," he told me. "I believe in people. I believe a miracle is coming." (Photo by Mark Patinkin)

"Muslim, Jewish, Christian," says another shopkeeper named Nasser, "the best thing is we live together."

I continue past the Church of the Holy Sepulchre, built 1,700 years ago by the Roman Emperor Constantine on the spot where Jesus was laid to rest and then rose. Opposite its courtyard is the Mosque of Omar, from the 1400s, and close to both, of course, the Western Wall itself. Jerusalem is a true convergence.

A Yeshiva student walks by in a bit of a hurry, saying he's on his way to study Talmud. Just one question then—what does he think of the war?

"The people of King David," he says, "are fighting for our land."

As he rushes on, I turn into the noted Zak's Antiquities shop, its proprietor, Zak Mishriki telling me he has weathered things by selling online as well as here.

"Tourism is a sensitive industry in this crazy country," says Zak.

Is he Muslim or Christian?

"It's a difficult question during the war," he says. Which tells you more than if he'd answered.

What does he think of the conflict?

"It's the outcome of religion," says Zak. For too long, faiths have fought.

One challenge, he tells me, is there is no shared view of the war. Being multilingual, Zak reads news in Arabic, Hebrew and English, and each has a different version.

His family has called Jerusalem home for four centuries, but he only recently became an Israeli citizen.

What was he before that?

He had Jordanian nationality even though he's never been to Jordan. And again I see how complicated it is here.

Zak offers another example of that: there are Jews here whose ancestors arrived from Sanaa in the 1800s, and if you ask who they are, they'll first say Yemenis, although Yemen is now Israel's enemy.

But Zak is glad to call Jerusalem home.

"It's less crazy than Europe soon," he says.

Soon? Does he mean with Islamic extremism emerging there?

"And right wing too," he says. "Here, we're trying to coexist."

The comment brings up an often-overlooked truth. Streets around the world are full of protests over this war, but in Israel, despite having two million Arab citizens, it is comparatively quiet. The rallies that do happen are Jews protesting Benjamin Netanyahu's government, many of them bitterly. But it says something about Jerusalem that in spring of 2024, U.S. campuses were in greater upheaval.

As I walked through the Old City's Greek Patriarchate, a reminder of Jerusalem's confluence of religions, a Greek Priest looked through an ancient doorway, declining to chat, but posing in an evocative tableau. (Photo by Mark Patinkin)

When folks ask Zak's background, does he say he's an Israeli or Palestinian?

"I say Jerusalemite," says Zak. "To avoid myself from the politics."

As for the war, he puts it in history's context.

"We have seen what happened with the Crusaders, with the Caliphates," he says, "we have seen a lot."

And now it is happening again, yet another war on the same soil that has experienced more than perhaps any other place.

I buy some items from Zak—he was kind enough to help me in my work; how could I not help him in his? Then I move on to the nearby Greek Orthodox enclave, at one point pausing by some intriguing history—the world's oldest tattoo shop, called Razzouk, its forebears having inked the skin of Crusaders during the 1300s.

As I continue through the area's Greek patriarchate, I notice an ancient iron doorway, a smallish opening reminding of what one might find in a ship. A white-bearded Greek Orthodox priest appears in black, declining to speak, but happy to pose from inside in a tableau evocative of the ancient city. The Greek Patriarchate, which began after the time of Jesus, faced challenges when the Romans destroyed Jerusalem in the year 70, then found renewal in the fourth century's time of Byzantine emperors. It is the story of this place, peoples falling and rising over the millennia, but somehow, impossibly, enduring.

As I walk, the feel around me is identical to when I was in the Old City 33 years before, a time I had a pair of extraordinary encounters which echo today—encounters with two of Jerusalem's highest figures of faith.

First—the Mufti.

To see him, I entered through the Damascus gate, down a flavorful Arab bazaar, at last arriving at the entrance of the Dome of the Rock grounds. After an Israeli soldier checked my bags, I emerged into the enormous stone courtyard, featuring the Al-Aqsa Mosque by its southern wall, and at its center, the great golden

Dome—shrine to the spot Muhammad ascended to heaven.

In an office only yards away, I met Muhammad Said Al Jamal Al Rivi, the Deputy Mufti in charge of these buildings. He had a gray beard and offered strong coffee. I asked him to tell me what Jerusalem means to the Palestinian people.

"It is everything," he said. Jerusalem embodies all they believe in.

And this site?

"Everything on this site is holy," said the Mufti. "Every stone is a holy stone. Every tree. The Prophets walked on these stones. The Martyrs. From Abraham until Jesus until Muhammad."

Would he ever accept that this ground—and all Jerusalem— should be shared with the Jews?

"If I say yes," he tells me, "I am standing against history and logic. It's a city for Muslims. That does not mean we cannot allow other people to practice their religion. But this should be a Palestinian city, an Islamic city."

The Jews say it's their city.

"Let them say what they want to say—they are saying they are the chosen people, that God does not create anyone but the Jews and all the world must be as servants of the Jewish people. It is not true."

How deep in him is this Dome of the Rock acreage?

He tells me he could not survive without this place. No Palestinian could. He loves to simply walk on the stones of the court-yard—to walk and to pray. He does it every day. It is part of his soul.

And now the rabbi.

It is astonishing to see how two of the planet's holiest places bump against each other so directly. The rabbi was in a space excavated next to the Western Wall below the ground where I met the Mufti.

His name was Shlomo Getz and his job mirrored the Mufti's: he oversees the Jews' most sacred sites. Even their two faces were similar—same beard, and eyes of studied piousness.

I asked how he, as a Jew, views Jerusalem.

"All of Israel is holy," he said. "Jerusalem is holier. It is the holiest place in the world."

Does he respect that this is holy ground to Muslims?

"For the Christians, also," Rabbi Getz said; Jerusalem is the land of Jesus. "But does that nullify our biblical right to this land?" Other religions have many holy cities. For Jews, this is the only one.

I asked if Jews and Muslims can coexist?

Jews, he says, have already made compromises. Where the Dome sits, he says, Solomon's temple once sat.

"But we've given up our right to go there."

I asked where he came from.

"Tunisia," he said—in 1948, the year of Israel's rebirth. But he had dreamt of coming here since childhood.

Couldn't he have been as good a Jew in Tunis?

"You can learn Torah anywhere, but you can only feel like a complete Jew in Israel."

Many of his words echoed the Mufti's. Every step he takes here is on holy ground, said the rabbi—this is where King David himself walked.

I asked if he'd show me where he prays; he was honored to. We descended into a kind of catacomb—an old underground Roman Street. Finally, we were at a small synagogue, a cool, dim chamber. The benches faced a barrier of great stones that were part of the Western Wall itself.

The rabbi said he has prayed here many thousands of times, but each session feels as if it's his first. The stones are like a wife and child, he said—they are part of him.

By the door, I noticed a plaque with names of soldiers who fell trying to reclaim this ground in the war of 1967. One of them was the son of Rabbi Shlomo Getz.

Now he approached this more private part of the wall and touched it.

As I watched him, I was picturing the Mufti, praying above on its other side.

>» «<

My last night in Israel on that trip, I was in a cab heading back to my hotel after a dinner when my Palestinian driver asked if I would like to take a scenic route. He stopped at a point high above the old city so we could walk to a public overlook and take in all of it. This is his city, he said; he was proud of it, and honored to share it.

The moment reminded me of a talk I had with an Israeli doctor.

"You ask me why I could never leave Israel?" the doctor said. "This city, that's why. And it's not because of the Bible; I'm not religious. It's something else. It has to just...happen to you. It's the smell, the stones, the trees. Very early in the morning, there is a specific light in Jerusalem I've never seen anywhere else, a kind of purple. I could never leave this city."

For long minutes, I stood with my Palestinian cab driver, the two of us simply gazing at the heart of Jerusalem, to many the world's most soulful skyline.

"So beautiful," my new Palestinian friend said. "Have you ever seen anything so beautiful?"

At last, in this place of war and division, I found a corner of hope. Ora Balha, raised Jewish, and her Muslim husband Ihab Balha, now run one of the few mixed-faith schools in Israel, called Orchards of Abraham, in Jaffa. "We can't give up," Ora told me. "Even when there's so much pain. We don't have a choice. These are our children." (Photo by Mark Patinkin)

TWENTY-ONE

A GLIMPSE OF HOPE

As this journey to Israel, the West Bank and Gaza reaches its end, I've learned a difficult truth. Because of Oct. 7, and the war, the divide between Palestinian and Jew is perhaps as wide as it's ever been, a remarkable statement given their difficult history.

Many Israelis once for peace now doubt they have a partner for it. And Palestinian anger over Gaza's devastation has hardened hearts.

Which is why in this final chapter, I offer a glimpse of hope: a rare school where both Jewish and Arab children share space, and life, and just maybe, sow seeds of more of that.

It is owned and run by a mixed couple—of course—and you can't help but smile when you meet them.

Ora, 47, the Jewish one, has the vibe of 1970s counterculture, and her Muslim husband, Ihab Balha, 53, even more so, with his white robe and salt-and-pepper hair tied back in what would be a ponytail if it weren't so bushy.

Ora's father didn't speak to her for years after she married an Arab. As for Ihab, he was raised to hate the Jew.

But across that divide, the two have bonded as kindred souls, and in their own odyssey, saw a model to be shared. This school of theirs that I am visiting now, this extraordinary place in Jaffa, has become their life's work.

It is called the Orchard of Abraham's school, and, despite its ideals of peace, let me start with the difficult reality they must navigate in Israel in 2024: the first spaces Ora wanted to show me were their new bomb shelters.

Together, they cost $400,000, but her primary mission is to ensure that the children are safe, and now they will be. The shelters are located throughout the school's buildings, and as we walk to see one, I ask where the idea for this unusual place came from.

Their firstborn child.

They named him Nur, and the world being what it is, they realized that no matter how hard they worked to teach acceptance of the other, it wouldn't be enough if their son didn't live it. The idea was to send him to a mixed school in Jaffa, except there were none there, and few in the country.

So Ora and Ihab decided to start one, and today, it is K-through-2, with an astonishing 55 staffers and 220 kids—60 percent Jewish and 40 percent Arab.

And now we're in its newest shelter, a prefab metal one lowered here by crane the day before. Ora tells me they also have a retrofitted kitchen space recently hardened with 30 extra centimeters of cement. I ask how many kids can fit inside each.

Ora smiles. As many as you can and still shut the door. When sirens go off, there is no such thing as being at capacity.

I tell Ora it's an amusing contrast to see a peace-and-love person so proud of a bomb shelter.

"We don't want a war," she explains, "but our children need to be safe."

That gets me asking if things have gotten harder for her mission of coexistence since Oct. 7. There's so much hatred now. Has it affected the kids?

No, she says—if you start young, they accept each other, no matter what's happening around them.

"We can't give up," she tells me, "even when there's so much pain. We don't have a choice."

Then she says simply: "These are our children."

I ask if the shelters have been used often.

Oh, many times, especially their older shelter. Early in the war, there were missile attacks on Jaffa every day. The car of one of the teachers was hit.

The war has touched them in many ways. A Palestinian staffer lost her uncle, his wife and their three children in Gaza. Ora's husband, Ihab, lost the son of a cousin there. And Orchard's Jewish families have friends among the Oct. 7 dead, as well as sons serving in the war.

In my weeks here and on the West Bank, this is the first community I've found that includes, within it, people on both sides mourning war losses, and you sense there is bonding over that.

With the tour finished, I sit with Ora and Ihab and ask how they met.

It was at a retreat with a 1960s sensibility—a Zen-like space in the Sinai, unfancy bungalows by the water with few amenities. The two noticed each other at a nightly bonfire, a Jewish woman and Arab man. As for what happened next, it sounds like an exaggeration, but they really did get married the next day.

"My father didn't speak to me for two years," says Ora. "It took him 10 years to be ready to meet Ihab."

What happened when he did?

"He saw Ihab didn't have a tail. He met the person instead of the label."

As she tells me the story, Ihab, sitting next to her, smiles serenely. I ask about his long, white robe, which gives him the look of the kind of guru the Beatles studied under. He says it's called a jalabiya, and its tranquility reflects who Ihab is.

Their son Nur—the one they founded the school for, and whose name is Arabic for "light"—is now 16. They have two other sons, 14 and 9.

I ask what they're raising them as. Ora answers simply.

"Humans."

Ora Balha stood with Amal Siksek, a teacher who helped her create the mixed faith school that both have embraced as their life's work. Amal uses a Hebrew phrase to describe the mission there - tikkun olam. It means repairing the world. (Photo by Mark Patinkin)

I assumed Ihab had been brought up in an accepting Muslim household, but it was the opposite.

"I grew up in a family that taught us to hate the Jew," he said.

His father lost two brothers in the 1948 war, was in a refugee camp at age 14 and was deeply angry. Ihab absorbed the same.

How did he overcome it?

A very long journey, he says—which is why they do the work they do. Bridging the Arab-Jewish divide is a process.

Since the school is about unwalled spaces instead of closed classrooms, we were talking near a gathering of kids. Ora brings me over to them to speak with Amal Siksek, in hijab, one of the original teachers who helped them found Orchard 16 years ago.

What drew her to this work?

"A child is born as pure," Amal says. This place seeks to hold onto that.

Although Arab, she uses a Jewish phrase to describe Orchard's mission: tikkun olam. It means repairing the world. Indeed, many parts of this region are broken, but not this school.

As I prepare to say goodbye, Ihab asks what brought me to them.

I tell him I'd mostly come to the Middle East to cover the war. But at least on one day, I wanted to write about hope.

He nods and holds my gaze.

"Inshalla."

As I begin to walk out, I pass a play area. There are about 25 kids together, Arab and Jewish.

I decide to pause and count how many there are of each.

But I cannot tell one from the other.

»» ««

ACKNOWLEDGMENTS

I was at home in Providence in December of 2023 when I got a text from Charlie Bakst, my newspaper's former political columnist, who knows everyone. He told me a retired dentist named Bob Ducoff would call to ask if I wanted to join a three-day Rhode Island mission to Israel as a reporter.

I hadn't heard about the trip, but I'd been writing about the war from afar, and it seemed a pretext to cover it on the ground through local folks at the scene. That's how this book began.

I ended up staying with the mission just one day, then going off on my own to report, extending my time to a week, then two, and finally almost three. I owe a thanks to Charlie and Bob for that text and phone call.

Medium sized newspapers don't have budgets for such trips anymore, so I paid my own way, but I know of few publications of any size that would have showcased my work the way the Providence Journal did—13 long stories in 14 days, written as a personal odyssey.

For that, I owe a thanks to Lynne Sullivan, my executive editor, who saw a role for a paper like ours to bring a different perspective to a global story. Thanks also to my immediate editors, Will Richmond, Kurt Mayer and Kathy Hill, who shepherded my daily dispatches under the gun.

As I tried to set things up in advance, I got invaluable help from an unexpected cadre of colleagues. It turns out there's a bit of a

Rhode Island journalist mafia in Israel.

From the States, I got onto a big chat group of Israel-based press members, asking for suggestions of a "fixer"—a guide and translator. I heard from Robby Berman, who is related to the prominent Rhode Island Hassenfeld family, founders of the Hasbro toy company. Robby drove me to the interviews I did, translating both Arabic and Hebrew, and pointed out things I might have missed, like bullet scars from 1948 on the Old City's Jaffa Gate.

On that same chat group, I got a text from Jack Mukand, a Jerusalem-based journalist with a focus on the West Bank, who introduced himself in a private message by saying, "You were my Little League coach." Jack, a Brown grad, helped me with many connections.

So did Allison Kaplan Sommer, a prominent writer with the Israeli daily, *Haaretz*. She's also from my home state of Rhode Island, and when I messaged that I was heading to Israel, I got an email from her mom telling me to look her up. I'm glad I did.

Lazar Berman of the *Times of Israel* is yet another Jerusalem journalist who grew up in my Providence neighborhood. He was a valuable resource, even letting me borrow his helmet and bullet proof vest the night before I went into Gaza with the IDF.

Plans seldom come together smoothly on a reporting trip like this, and I often feared I was failing. But I was buoyed by a former colleague, Wayne Worcester, a gifted writer and journalism professor emeritus at the University of Connecticut, who sent daily emails coaching me through the game. His feedback was hugely helpful.

I got similar support from many family members, including my brothers and adult nephews and nieces. It can be lonely in the field, but their belief in my work in real time got me through. So did texts from my three 30-something children, Ariel, Alex and Zach—as well as my "fourth child" Nikki, and my partner Claudia. I felt all of them were with me on the journey.

To everyone listed, and with apologies to any I left out, a deep thank you for being on my wing.

ABOUT THE AUTHOR

MARK PATINKIN has been writing a column for the Providence Journal for over 45 years, starting in 1979 at age 26. Around 6,000 columns later, he is still at it.

Patinkin has written about famine in Africa, religious conflict in Northern Ireland, India and Beirut, and recently, the Gaza War. He covered the collapse of communism in Eastern Europe, where he was arrested by the secret police in Stalinist Romania for trying to interview a dissident and expelled from the country.

Closer to home, he has done columns on the pain of his unexpected divorce, brought readers into the operating room for his own recent kidney cancer surgery, and shared the hard journey of losing his father to dementia. He is also known for a lighter touch, including columns about his adult kids being embarrassed he tucks Polo shirts into cargo shorts while wearing high white crew socks and New Balance sneakers.

In addition to "The Holy Land at War," Patinkin has written "An African Journey," "The Silent War," about the world's most competitive companies, and "Just the Way He Was Before," about a boy who lost both legs to bacterial meningitis but went on to play ice hockey.

Patinkin was a finalist for the Pulitzer Prize in International Reporting and was recently named columnist of the year for Gatehouse Media, now Gannett.

He won three New England Emmy Awards for weekly "video columns" for Rhode Island's ABC affiliate.

He has received honorary degrees from both Rhode Island College and Johnson and Wales University.

Patinkin graduated from Middlebury College and lives in Providence.

»» ««

MARK PATINKIN CAN BE REACHED AT
MARKPATINKIN1@GMAIL.COM

Made in the USA
Monee, IL
22 August 2024

64342621R00154